KNOCK-OUT BLACKJACK

KNOCK-OUT
Blackjack

The Easiest Card-Counting
System Ever Devised

Olaf Vancura, Ph.D.
&
Ken Fuchs

HUNTINGTON PRESS
Las Vegas, Nevada

Knock-Out Blackjack

Published by
Huntington Press
3687 South Procyon Avenue
Las Vegas, Nevada 89103
(702) 252-0655 Phone
(702) 252-0675 Fax
e-mail: books@huntingtonpress.com

ISBN 0-929712-31-5

Cover Design: Maile Austraw
Interior Design: Jason Cox

Printing History
1st Edition—September 1998
Reprinted—May 2000, April 2001, June 2003

To all who have been knocked out by the casinos...

Acknowledgments

The authors are indebted to Andy Bloch, Anthony Curtis, Michael Dalton, Peter Griffin, J. P. Massar, Donald Schlesinger, Ralph Stricker, Edward O. Thorp, Zeb Vancura, and Dick Vannelli for reading, commenting on, and contributing to preliminary versions of this manuscript.

We also thank Paul Bauer, Geoff Talvola, and John Spaulding for assistance in the confirmation of K-O simulation results and for valuable feedback in initial field-trial applications of the K-O technique.

We are grateful to our wives Kathy and Tracy for putting up with grown men who behave like kids when discussing blackjack. You are real "Knock-Outs" to us.

Table of Contents

Preface

There is the notion, often put forth by the casinos, that card counting requires a mind like Albert Einstein's, together with a memory tantamount to that of a Pentium computer. Nonsense! And yet, the vast majority of blackjack players do not presently count cards.

We have invented a new, simple, scientific technique of beating casino blackjack, which we call the Knock-Out (K-O) system. You don't need a math degree to be able to participate; virtually anyone who has ever applied the principles of the basic strategy (and can count up and down by ones) will be able to put K-O to good use.

But don't let the simplicity of the Knock-Out system fool you. K-O's power compares favorably with all the proven card-counting systems. This has been verified not only through simulations of billions of computer-generated hands, but also by the actual play of card-counting teams throughout the United States.

After reading this book, you too will have the knowledge necessary to successfully "Knock-Out" the casinos in the game of blackjack.

Round 1

A Historical Perspective of Card Counting

It isn't so much the money. It never has
been. The big part of winning is being able
to feel the way David must have felt when
he killed Goliath.
—Edward O. Thorp, BEAT THE DEALER

The popularity of gaming continues unabated. This year, gamblers will wager more than $400 billion in casinos and state lotteries in the United States.[1] To place this in context, on a yearly basis, the average American wagers about $1,600!

And in virtually each of the hundreds of casinos spread throughout the nation, the number-one table game is blackjack. From the Las Vegas Strip to the Atlantic City Boardwalk and every gambling jurisdiction in between, blackjack reigns supreme as the king of casino table games. Nearly $90 billion a year is wagered at blackjack tables. This corresponds to an annual wagering level of some $350 per citizen on this one game alone.

And how do we do against the mighty house? Not so well, it turns out. Annually, American casinos collectively win almost $2 billion from blackjack, with a typical blackjack table

---

[1] Statistics based on the *Ernst & Young Compilation of the Gaming Industry.*

realizing some $250,000 in profits.

Given these substantial losses by the wagering public, it is perhaps all the more amazing to learn that a skillful black-jack player can beat the casinos at their own game. With proper play, blackjack *can*, in almost all situations, quite legally be beaten. This is accomplished by a technique called card count-ing. The idea behind card counting is simple: a player uses information about cards already played to determine the favorability of the remaining pack. Not too hard. To date, however, this concept has been difficult to implement.

We'll attempt to remedy this in the pages that follow. But first, let's take a quick look back at some of the key mile-stones in the history of blackjack. In particular, we'll focus on attempts to beat the game over the past half-century or so.

THE ORIGINS OF CARD COUNTING

As with many of life's pleasures that are now taken for granted, the exact origin of the game of blackjack is unclear.[2] Several countries have laid claim to (originating) the game of twenty-one. It may have been an offshoot of the Spanish "one and thirty," in existence since at least the 16th century.

In any event, twenty-one was introduced into American gaming halls shortly after the turn of the 20th century. After a few years, houses began to introduce a variation wherein a hand consisting of an ace of spades and a black jack garnered a bonus. This gave birth to the name blackjack. The game spread to Nevada in the 1930s, and by 1950 blackjack had surpassed roulette as the second most popular game behind craps.

---

[2] See, for example, *Scarne's New Complete Guide to Gambling* by John Scarne, 1974, Simon & Schuster.

To be sure, though, at this time almost all blackjack players performed poorly and lost quickly. Though the game had been offered in casinos for decades, it was played crudely. Players typically employed very conservative strategies, often refusing to hit stiff totals of 12 through 16, which could potentially bust with the draw of another card.

However, in the second half of the century, things began to change. In 1953, a group of four Army mathematicians began working on a study of the game. After three years of painstaking calculations (the computer age had not yet dawned), Baldwin, Cantey, Maisel, and McDermott published the first blackjack basic strategy in 1956. In "The Optimum Strategy in Blackjack," published in the *Journal of the American Statistical Association*, Baldwin et al. described what they termed the "optimum strategy," now commonly referred to as the basic strategy (see Chapter 2).

The strategy they recommended was very unlike the common wisdom of the day. In their paper the group noted that, "The 'optimum strategy' differs substantially from the published strategies of card experts and the usual style of play in the casinos."

In addition to presenting an accurate basic strategy for the game of blackjack, the Baldwin group reported several other important findings. First, they determined that with proper strategy, the player has a better expectation in blackjack than in any other casino game. Though the group originally calculated an expectation of –0.6% (the player is expected to lose 0.6% of total initial wagers), they later revised this upward to –0.3% (the actual expectation for the single-deck game they analyzed was nearly 0.0%). Before that time, the prevailing "best" strategy (attributed to Culbertson et al.) yielded a rather dismal expectation of –3.6%.

Another major find of the Baldwin group was the notion that certain dealer upcards are favorable to the player, while others are unfavorable. That is, the player's chances of winning a hand are dependent on the dealer's upcard. Of this, the group wrote summarily, "The player's conditional expectation, given the dealer's upcard, shows considerable variability." This is a very important concept and one we shall explain shortly.

At about the same time, others began studying the game.[3]

THE WISDOM OF YESTERYEAR

Today's experienced players might be amused by the strategies employed by blackjack players of decades earlier. Below is a sampling of the Baldwin group's overview of prevailing 1950s' play.

On hitting and standing: "Few experienced players recommend standing on a total of 13 under any circumstances, and standing on 12 would be completely out of the question."

On splitting: "Splitting 8s, for example, is seldom seen in the casinos, while splitting 10s and face cards is not uncommon."

On doubling down: "Doubling down is not recommended by any writers. Doubling down is not common in the casinos and, in particular, the idea of doubling down on soft hands probably does not occur to most players. One may even go so far as to say that doubling down is the most neglected and underrated aspect of blackjack strategy."

---

[3] For a more detailed description, see for example Allan Wilson's *The Casino Gambler's Guide*, 1965, Harper & Row.

In 1956, Richard Epstein created a "decision matrix" that demonstrated the percentage difference in expectation for appropriate hitting, standing, splitting, and doubling down. In conjunction with estimates of initial two-card hands, Epstein calculated the basic strategy expectation to be –0.14%. By 1959, Robert Lea had encoded a computer to calculate the basic strategy. He obtained a more correct estimate of the expectation at –0.01%.

To differing degrees, these bright investigators had begun unraveling the secrets of blackjack. They recognized that proper basic strategy made blackjack almost an even game. What's more, some of them even had an inkling that the game could be beaten with additional information.

Indeed, the understanding of the game was revolutionized once again when a young scientist named Edward O. Thorp—"a veritable supernova," according to Wilson—burst onto the scene. Dr. Thorp came across the results of the Baldwin group shortly after their article was published. For an upcoming trip to Las Vegas, Thorp wrote the basic strategy rules on a small card. Upon arriving at a casino, he "pur-

---

THE CULBERTSON STRATEGY

Below is a sampling of the strategy espoused by the Culbertson team, as reported by the Baldwin group.

Hitting and standing: Stand on 14 or more if the dealer's upcard is 6 or less. Stand on 16 or more with a dealer upcard of 7 or more. Stand on all soft totals of 18 or more.

Splitting: Only split aces.

Doubling down: Never double down.

chased ten silver dollars" (the good old days) in order to try out the system.

Thorp writes in *Beat the Dealer*,[4] "In a few moments the slowness of my play and the little card in my palm amused and attracted bystanders. The dealer could not conceal his scorn." He adds, "These sentiments were soon laced with pity when these people saw, further, the details of the way in which I played." However, some twenty minutes (and a seven-card hand totaling 21) later when Thorp still had not exhausted his meager stake, he noted, "The amusement and patronizing attitude of some bystanders changed to respect [and] attentiveness."

After his trip, Thorp began studying the game in earnest. He recognized that although the Baldwin group had made great strides in the understanding of blackjack, they apparently had overlooked an important facet of the game. Baldwin and his colleagues wrote that their strategy was "developed under the assumption that the player does not have the time or inclination to utilize the information available in the hands of the players preceding him." They further surmised, "There are tremendous difficulties in using this information except in an intuitive, non-scientific manner."

Thorp took exception to these statements. He became convinced that, with proper play, a skilled player would be able to *beat* the game. That is, the tables would be turned, and the player would have a positive expectation. Hence, over time, the lowly player would be expected to beat the mighty house.

As is true of many inventors, Thorp had the wisdom to appreciate the importance of what many took for granted. For unlike the Declaration of Independence, which states that "all men are created equal," the fact is that all cards (in blackjack) are *not*.

Thorp realized that certain cards were favorable to the

---

[4] Edward O. Thorp, *Beat the Dealer*, 1962, Random House.

player and others to the dealer. The Baldwin group had shown that this was true for the *present* cards in play (those the dealer or player were now holding). But Thorp took the concept a giant leap forward. He reasoned that, in general, among the *remaining* cards (those as yet still unplayed), an excess of certain card denominations would be beneficial to the player, while an excess of others would help the dealer.

And thus the modern system of card counting was conceived. Sequential hands are dependent events. Information on cards already played yields information about the cards still remaining. If the relative abundance of these remaining good and bad cards could be identified, then the player's advantage or disadvantage could be estimated.

Thorp made good use of his access to computers, and several intense years of study and simulation ensued. At last, in 1961 he presented the exciting results at an American Mathematical Society meeting. In 1962 he published the first card-counting treatise on blackjack, the best-selling *Beat the Dealer*. In it were the words that would send the casino industry reeling: "In the modern casino game of blackjack, the player can gain a consistent advantage over the house by using the strategy that is presented in this book."

Thorp's book eventually created a sensation, riding a wave of popularity to the *New York Times* bestseller list. And why not? For, as Bryce Carlson wrote in *Blackjack for Blood*,[5] "Here was a book, written by a respected mathematician from a prominent university, that contained the secret formula for making free money—or so some thought."

Blackjack's popularity soared. Major magazines ran articles describing how the game could be beaten. Consider the accolades in the following excerpt from *Life*: "Thorp does not cheat. But Thorp cannot lose. Humans have been betting

---

[5] Bryce Carlson, *Blackjack for Blood*, 1994, CompuStar Press.

on games of chance since the dawn of history, but Thorp must be considered the greatest system player of all time."

Not surprisingly, casinos first reacted with anxiety. Commented Carlson, "If the man in the street was overreacting a bit, it was nothing compared to the hysteria that seized the casino industry. Suddenly, they had nightmares of thousands of trained counters swooping down on them like swarms of merciless locusts, devouring every hundred dollar bill in sight." This frame of mind led many casinos to change the rules of the game to make it harder for players to win.

That situation didn't last long, as Lance Humble and Carl Cooper wrote in *The World's Greatest Blackjack Book*,[6] "Too many players refused to play blackjack with these unfavorable rules, and the win volumes dropped off dramatically."

To bring players back, casinos were soon forced to capitulate and reinstate the old rules. After some tense days, the casinos began to relax when they realized that though many people thought they could beat the game, few actually could. Remarked Humble and Cooper, "The casinos soon realized that they had nothing to fear. The publicity that Thorp's book provided turned out to be a boon." Why? "The players kept losing at exactly the same rate as before, only now there were more of them."

Blackjack's popularity continues in high stride today. Apparently the lure of playing a game that is *potentially* beatable is sufficient for most people, who somehow believe that Dame Fortune will smile on them despite their inadequacies in play.

But these people miss the point. It's not enough to merely show up to a game that *can* be beaten. One also needs to play properly. It's similar to a college midterm exam on which you want to get an A grade. It's a given that you'll show up to

---

[6] Lance Humble & Carl Cooper, *The World's Greatest Blackjack Book*, 1980, Doubleday.

take the exam, but you must show up prepared to earn the A. But putting in work, practice, and patience to learn to play well, Carlson argued, "is not what the people were looking

---

THREE SIDES OF THE SAME COIN

The old adage that there are two sides to every story certainly applies to a recap of the fallout from the publication of *Beat the Dealer*. Below is a sampling of spin (or perhaps revisionist history) provided by the feuding sides in the casino/card-counter battle.

The card counter's side: Carlson writes, in *Blackjack for Blood*, "Their paranoia out of control, the Las Vegas casinos snapped! On April Fool's Day 1964, the casinos on the Las Vegas Strip changed the rules of blackjack, the first (and only) time the rules of a major casino game had ever been significantly altered. And the changes were drastic. Doubling down was restricted to two-card totals of 11 only, and a pair of aces could no longer be split. The effect on the average player was disastrous, and play at the tables all but vanished."

The casino's side: A "suave PR man," in a *Newsweek* article dated April 13, 1964, indicates that the operators eliminated the "fringe benefits" of the game, namely "the right" to double most bets and to split hands of two aces.

A third side to the story? Thorp's nonchalant reply (in the same *Newsweek* article) to all the hoopla: "Instead of five hours, now I'll have to play seven to make the same money."

for. They preferred instead to continue in their old, uninformed ways." Humble and Cooper have said that most people who bought Thorp's book simply did not take the time to master card counting.

Of course, it didn't help when supposed experts muddied the waters with misinformation. As soon as the diligent work of an esteemed scientist became public, self-proclaimed card-counting experts came out of the woodwork claiming supreme knowledge of the subject. (It's amazing how that seems to work. It's reminiscent of the developments in the first part of the 20th century shortly after Albert Einstein published his general theory of relativity. The great scientist Arthur Eddington was in West Africa observing an eclipse in an attempt to perform a test of Einstein's ideas. A reporter interviewing Eddington commented, "It is said that the general theory is so complicated that there are but three men in the world who can understand it." To which Eddington replied, "Who's the third?") John Scarne, for example, labeled card counting "chicanery," and argued that it required unusual natural ability. "You can't remember all the exposed cards dealt to a full table of players," Scarne wrote. While the statement is certainly true for most people, it is irrelevant and misleading. The Thorp system didn't require the memorization of all the exposed cards. Quite the contrary; Thorp recognized that this was beyond the means of mere mortals and designed a system that could be implemented by everyday folks.

Wilson also worried about the agendas of some blackjack writers, and commented in *The Casino Gambler's Guide* that those associated with casino management might "purposely give some bum steers." Even so, such attempts did little to dampen the impact of Thorp's findings.

Knowing that *Beat the Dealer* would release the genie from the bottle, Thorp wrote, "Eventually, when the strategy we outline becomes general practice, casinos may change the game or discontinue it."

Clearly, the game has changed markedly. In the 1960s, casinos typically used single decks and dealt through to the end. Whenever the pack was exhausted, often mid-hand, the dealer would reshuffle the discards and continue dealing. The burn card was shown to all players. No casino today would dare deal the game of the 1960s. Today, typically one-quarter of the pack is cut off and these cards are never brought into play. In fact, it's now a cardinal sin for a dealer to run out of cards; in some casinos this is cause for immediate dismissal.

Since the publication of *Beat the Dealer*, many other experts have refined Thorp's method and developed new systems. Indeed, this process began almost as the book first hit the bookstores. It was the dawn of the computer age, which was certainly a boon to the early system developers.

As we'll see in Chapter 3, the fundamental concept behind modern card-counting systems is to assign a value to each particular card. The value is a measure of how much the card's removal changes our expectation for the game. The sign (plus or minus) of the value represents whether the card's removal helps or hurts us.

Thorp, in the original edition of *Beat the Dealer*, presented several methods for beating the game, including the popular and simple Ten Count. He also revealed the first point-count system, which he called the "Ultimate Count." Unfortunately, to take full advantage of the multiple-level *ultimate* technique, the player had to keep three running counts in his head, one of which could jump up by 11 or down by 9 on the turn of a single card. This full-blown system proved a bit much for most players.

One of the first to try to simplify card counting was Claude Shannon, who in 1961 proposed a simple set of count values, which later became known as High-Low. Thorp and Shannon quickly recognized the worthiness of the High-Low values, which were adopted and made popular by Harvey Dubner in 1963.

The High-Low count is a single-level count, often referred to as level 1. That is to say, all cards are assigned a point count equal to +1, 0, or –1 (see Chapter 3). Julian Braun took the premise and, via computer, determined the correct betting and playing strategies to go along with the point-count values. This simplified card-counting system appeared in the second edition of Thorp's *Beat the Dealer*[7] in 1966.

A few years later in *Playing Blackjack as a Business,*[8] Lawrence Revere presented the High-Low, as well as a similar system that facilitated the so-called "true-count conversion" (more on this in chapter 3). To this day, the High-Low count is one of the most popular and successful systems, and is maintained by Dr. Stanford Wong in his excellent series of books.[9]

In 1968, Charles Einstein[10] suggested a somewhat different set of card-counting values, the key difference being the way in which aces were treated. The ace alone is unique in that it can take one of two values, either 1 or 11. For betting purposes, the ace typically acts as a high card and is very valuable to the player. However, once you're playing the hand and making strategic decisions on how to proceed, the ace usually acts like a low card. This chameleon-like nature of the ace has caused system developers and card counters considerable anguish over the years.

To circumvent this problem, Einstein proposed counting the ace as zero. Unlike Dubner, who counted aces the same as any other high-valued card (10, jack, queen, or king), Einstein kept them neutral and counted only small cards (3-6) vs. tens. Einstein also advocated keeping a separate count

---

[7] Edward O. Thorp, *Beat the Dealer*, 1966, Random House.

[8] Lawrence Revere, *Playing Blackjack as a Business*, 1969, Carol Publishing.

[9] See, for example, Stanford Wong, *Professional Blackjack*, 1994, Pi Yee Press.

[10] Charles Einstein, *How to Win at Blackjack*, 1968, Cornerstone Library.

of the ratio of aces to non-aces, and recommended strategic departures from the basic strategy depending on the prevailing excess or deficit of small cards.

Einstein's concept was later "refined and expanded" by Julian Braun, an anonymous Mr. G, and Drs. Lance Humble and Carl Cooper to become the Hi-Opt I system. A very readable treatment of the Hi-Opt I system can be found in Humble and Cooper's *The World's Greatest Blackjack Book.*

In 1979, Peter Griffin issued the first edition of *The Theory of Blackjack,*[11] in which he presented mathematical analyses

---

THE PROGRESSION OF FLOPS

The progression of computing power is an interesting story in its own right.

The Baldwin group collectively spent 12 man-years painstakingly calculating the basic strategy on electronic calculators, the major computation aid at the time.

In his studies, Thorp used a state-of-the-art IBM 704 mainframe computer. His FORTRAN programs enabled the machine to perform the equivalent of some 10,000 man-years of work. The executable time of an approximation was typically 10 minutes.

Today, with an increase of several orders of magnitude in computational power and speed, computer calculations of the same complexity can be done in seconds.

---

[11] Peter A. Griffin, *The Theory of Blackjack*, 1998, Huntington Press.

of many different facets of the game. The multiple editions of this landmark work have since served as the premier reference to blackjack. Many enterprising students of the game have applied Griffin's results to develop novel techniques to beat casino blackjack.

The trend in the 1980s first grew toward more complicated systems in an attempt to squeeze out every last advantage a player could possibly have. Ken Uston wrote of several systems, including the popular Uston Advanced Point Count (Uston APC).[12] Unfortunately, though the system performed admirably in computer simulations, the level-3 card-counting values were difficult to master. Uston later recanted and recommended the simpler Uston Advanced Plus-Minus.[13]

Bucking the trend toward complexity, Dr. John Gwynn Jr. and Jeffrey Tsai's paper "Multiparameter Systems for Blackjack Strategy Variation" was the first to study the effects of slight errors in the true count and their minimal impact on a count system's performance. (This concept was furthered by Arnold Snyder with the High-Low Lite and recently brought to some closure with the complementary work of this book's authors in their paper, "A Study of Index Rounding."[14])

Moving further to simplicity, Arnold Snyder wrote the progressive *Blackbelt in Blackjack*[15] in the early 80s, in which he introduced the first "unbalanced" point-count system for the entire game of blackjack, which he dubbed Red Seven. The Red Seven system was a breakthrough in simplicity, a

---

[12] See Ken Uston's *Million Dollar Blackjack*, 1981, Gambling Times. Note that this count was introduced by Peter Griffin and dubbed "Griffin 3."

[13] See Ken Uston's *Uston on Blackjack*, 1986, Barricade Books.

[14] Presented at the "10th International Conference on Gambling and Risk Taking," 1997, by Ken Fuchs and Olaf Vancura. See *Finding the Edge*, 1998, UNR Press.

[15] Arnold Snyder, *Blackbelt in Blackjack*, 1997, RGE Publishing.

pseudo level-1 system with all cards valued at +1, 0, or –1. Due to the unbalanced nature of the system, no true-count conversion, hence mental multiplication and division, is ever necessary (see Chapter 3 for a definition of unbalanced counts and true-count conversion). The only (minor) drawback to counting the Red Seven system, when compared to others, is that players need to keep track of the colors on all 7-valued cards.

Players use card-counting information to decide not only how much to bet, but also how to strategically play the ensuing hand. Snyder advocated the use of a greatly reduced strategy matrix. In this shortened form, players need only memorize a handful of strategic plays that potentially differ from the basic strategy. Although the Red Seven system was not fully developed for professional play, even the simplified form is quite capable of beating the game of blackjack. The Knock-Out system is predicated on many of the important principles introduced by Snyder.

In 1986, Don Schlesinger[16] was the first to exhaustively evaluate the relative merits of memorizing the card-counting entries associated with each of the many possible strategic plays. Up until that point, systems developers typically delivered strategy matrices with a hundred or more entries to be memorized. Schlesinger showed that memorizing just 18 of these plays, the so-called "Illustrious 18," afforded the card counter roughly 80% of the total possible gain!

Relatively recently, Bryce Carlson[17] introduced the Omega II system (independently developed, but similar to an earlier count presented by Richard Canfield). This level-2 system performs brilliantly and seems to be the choice of many young

---

[16] See Donald Schlesinger, *Attacking the Shoe*, in *Blackjack Forum*, September, 1986.

[17] Bryce Carlson, *Blackjack for Blood*, 1994, CompuStar Press.

whippersnappers aiming to maximize their expectation. However, the Omega II system requires managing not only level-2 counting values, but also a side count of aces and the true-count conversion. This puts it out of the league of casual players.

In theory at least, the most powerful system is the one with the highest player expectation, regardless of complexity. In practice, however, the systems with the best theoretical expectation are more complicated, leaving players more susceptible to error. It's a vicious cycle. Systems designed to enhance performance do so at a cost of increased complexity, which in turn detracts from performance, which defeats the original purpose.

Is there a way out of this self-defeating Catch 22? First, it's important to realize that most popular card-counting systems have relatively minor differences (in expectation) among them when compared to the different conditions the average person will encounter in casinos. That is to say, no matter which system you as a player use, your overall expectation will be governed not so much by the specific card-counting method you employ, but by the conditions under which you play (we will return to this subject later).

For casual players, this is and has almost always been true. But even professional card counters, unless they are already playing exclusively at games with the best possible conditions, have now changed course. The clear trend is toward simpler systems (to which the player is less error-prone) that perform nearly as well as their complicated counterparts. The simpler systems, too, make professionals less susceptible to fatigue (yes, playing blackjack is a job for some), allowing them to play longer, and hence, earn more.

And so it seems we may have come full circle.

The most popular counts today are, perhaps surprisingly, variations of the original point-count systems. For all the improvements and simplifications that have occurred in the last

35 years, card counting remains relatively inaccessible to most of us. There's simply too much to do, what with all the bells clanging, dealers talking, cocktail waitresses jiggling, pit bosses staring, eyes-in-the-sky watching, players chatting, and money changing hands.

So have we exhausted the possibilities? Has blackjack been milked for all it's worth? Thankfully no. Is there anything left for the rest of us? The answer is yes.

Necessity is the mother of invention, and the need for simplicity is the reason the Knock-Out method was conceived. We believe the Knock-Out system is, to date, the easiest professional-level card-counting system ever devised: a system capable of making better players out of almost all of us. The ease of play makes card counting "fun" for even the most serious player. And the simplicity does not come at the expense of performance. The K-O system is a top-caliber tool at your disposal. Let's get ready for round 2.

Round 2

The Basic Strategy

One of the characteristics of the basic strategy is that, by using it, you will be considerably 'luckier' than the average player.
—Edward O. Thorp, BEAT THE DEALER

Historically, the trend in blackjack card-counting books is to first describe the basic strategy, then proceed with the "good stuff." Wise men have said, "Lead, follow, or get the hell out of the way." Who are we to argue? Here we choose to foray along the path forged by our esteemed predecessors.

At this point, readers unfamiliar with the rules of blackjack are advised to consult Appendix I. Those unfamiliar with the jargon of blackjack will find Appendix II helpful in defining terms such as "hard" and "soft," among others.

Although you may be tempted to skip over this chapter and go straight for the "Knock-Out," so to speak, we urge you to reconsider.[18] The basic strategy is, after all, the foun-

---

[18] The experienced basic strategy player or card counter may wish to skip ahead and simply refresh his or her memory of the basic strategy table presented on pg. 28.

dation for any card-counting system. Indeed, especially for the Knock-Out system, a complete knowledge of the basic strategy is essential. Because of the unbalanced nature of the Knock-Out system, most of the gain from using K-O comes from making proper *betting* decisions, as opposed to *playing* decisions. With the K-O system, you will be making basic strategy plays at least 90% of the time!

What exactly is the basic strategy? The basic strategy is a system that maximizes performance *without* keeping track of the cards. Under the best of conditions, the expectation one achieves while using the basic strategy is nearly 0%, making blackjack almost an even game.

The basic strategy consists of a set of rules that the player should always follow. It's an objective system that assumes that the cards in play are from a freshly shuffled pack (of one or more decks). This is the optimal method of play with knowledge of only the cards the player is holding and the dealer's upcard (and perhaps information about the dealer's downcard, for example, when the upcard is an ace and the dealer doesn't have a natural, we know that there is a non-ten in the hole).

HOUSE ADVANTAGE VS. PLAYER ADVANTAGE

It's instructive to understand how the casino makes money at blackjack. Despite what well-meaning fellow players or pit bosses may tell you, the house has only one advantage over the player:

1. The player must act first, and if both the player and dealer bust, the dealer wins.

If this seems of limited consequence, realize that the average player busts some 15% of the time. To counter this disadvantage, the player has several potential advantages over the dealer:

1. The player receives a payment of 3 to 2 for naturals (the dealer is "paid" only 1 to 1 for his naturals).
2. The player is allowed to play his hand as he wishes (the dealer must hit or stand according to house rules).
3. The player can split two equally valued cards (the dealer cannot).
4. The player can double down (the dealer cannot).
5. The player can take insurance (the dealer cannot).
6. The player can, in some casinos, surrender his hand (the dealer cannot).

The basic strategy, then, seeks to take maximum advantage of these options available to the player.

THE DEALER'S PLAY

For security purposes, the casinos like all dealers to play their hands by a standard set of rules. Management prefers that dealers have no say whatsoever in how their hands are played. This avoids possible errors in judgment and precludes collusion between an unscrupulous dealer and player.

Because the house always plays in a fixed manner, we know exactly what to expect from the dealer. Let's take a closer look at the dealer's play.

In many casinos in the United States, the dealer keeps hitting until reaching a total of 17 or more. That is, once the dealer reaches 17, he must stop, regardless of what the players have as their totals. Other casinos offer a variation in which the dealer must continue to hit if holding a soft 17 (soft hands always contain an ace which counts as 11). In this case, the

BLACKJACK Fallacy

The object is to get to 21

Casino literature often mistakenly states that, "The object of the game is to get to a total of 21, or as close as possible, without exceeding 21." This is a misleading statement.

The true object of the game is to win, and to win you must beat the dealer's hand. It's true that having a hand whose value is close to, but does not exceed, a total of 21 means your chances of winning the hand are good. But often, the best strategy is to stand, despite the fact that your total is far from 21, especially when the dealer has a weak upcard. In such cases you are hoping the dealer will bust, whereby you win regardless of your total.

dealer must hit until reaching a total of 17 or more on hard hands, and 18 or more on soft hands. In some casinos, the hit-soft-17 rule is employed in single- or double-deck games, while the dealer stands on all 17s in multiple-deck games (the rule in force is usually specified on the table layout).

Since we know exactly how the dealer will play, cycling through all the possible card sequences allows us to obtain the dealer's theoretical distribution. Figures 1 and 2 were generated by this type of combinatorial analysis, assuming a pack of two freshly shuffled decks. We've chosen the 2-deck game for our examples because it serves as an "average" of the many games offered in casinos.

First, let's look at the theoretical final distribution of values for the dealer's hand. Looking at Figure 1, you can see that overall the dealer busts about 28% of the time, assuming we consider no information about the dealer's up-

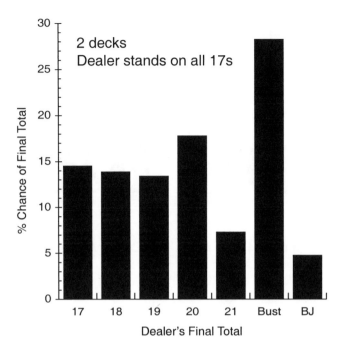

Figure 1: *The distribution of final values for the dealer's hand in a 2-deck blackjack game, assuming a freshly shuffled pack.*

card.[19] Additionally, the dealer will reach a pat hand (17 through 21) about 67% of the time, the remaining 5% or so accounted for by naturals.

In reality the dealer's final outcome is heavily dependent on the upcard. Via the same combinatorial analysis, we obtain Figure 2 (pgs. 24 and 25), which shows the distribution of dealer's final totals as a function of the upcard in a 2-deck game.

Note that the dealer is most likely to bust showing a 2, 3, 4, 5, or 6 as his upcard. However, under no circumstances

---

[19] That is, each of the thirteen possibilities from ace through king is equally likely.

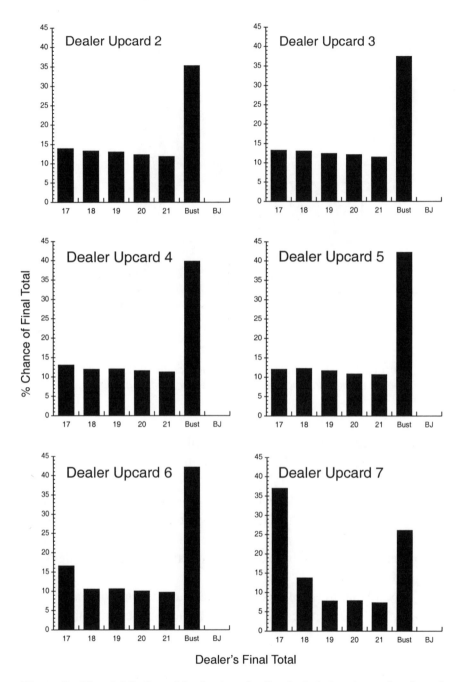

Figure 2: *The distribution of final values for the dealer's hand as a function of upcard, assuming a freshly shuffled 2-deck pack.*

does the dealer have as high as a 50% chance of busting. Although a 5 or 6 is commonly referred to as a "dealer's bust card," the smart money is still on the dealer to draw to a pat hand.

Furthermore, a dealer showing an upcard of 8 or more has less than a 25% chance of busting. With high-valued upcards such as a 9, ten, or ace, the dealer is very likely to make a good hand. For these reasons, we say that the dealer "shows weakness" with an upcard of 2 through 6, while the

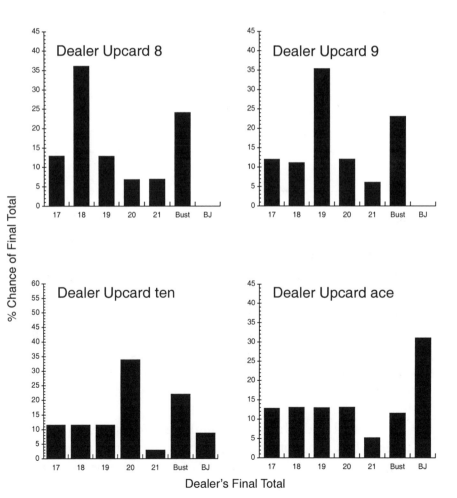

BLACKJACK Fallacy

A deuce is the dealer's ace

It's not uncommon to hear a dealer whose upcard is a 2 say something like, "Remember, a deuce is the dealer's ace." The remark is usually made as a player is about to decide whether or not to take another hit—the dealer's warning being that he is almost as likely to make a pat hand with a 2 as with an ace.

A glance back at the dealer-hand charts will verify that this is not true. The ace, far and away, is the strongest card for the dealer, while the 2 falls somewhere in the middle. With a 2 up, the dealer has about a 35% chance of busting. With an ace up, the chance is only about 12%. And with an ace showing, even when the dealer doesn't have a natural, the chance of busting is still only about 17%. Deuce, you're no ace.

---

dealer "shows strength" with an upcard of 9 or higher.

It's also worth noting the "break" that occurs between upcards of 2 through 6 and upcards of 7 through ace. In the former, the final distribution of dealer hands is similar and not a sensitive function of the upcard. In each case, the dealer's most likely outcome is to bust. In the latter, the final distribution is a fairly sensitive function of the upcard. In each case here, the dealer's most likely outcome is to achieve a hand equal to ten plus the upcard value. This has led to the mnemonic crutch that tells us to assume that "the dealer has a ten in the hole."

You will find it helpful to familiarize yourself with these figures. It is important to realize, for example, that the dealer is much more likely to reach a total of 20 if the upcard is a jack as opposed to a 5. On the other hand, the dealer is more likely to bust with an upcard of a 6 than with an upcard of an ace.

BASIC STRATEGY RULES

In principle, each basic strategy decision can be calculated by cycling through all the possible ways of playing a hand and choosing the one with the greatest expected return. This could be repeated for every possible set of playing conditions encountered to generate a different basic strategy for each possible blackjack variation encountered. While most basic strategies are created to apply specifically to either single or multiple decks, in practice, we have found it best to memorize one generic basic strategy table. This is because the gain in memorizing additional variations is very minimal, amounting to a total additional gain of roughly 0.03% overall.

In the Knock-Out system, we are striving for the best blend of simplicity and power. Hence, we recommend the use of the generic basic strategy, which is applicable in all games, from hand-held single decks to 8-deck shoes. The complete generic basic strategy chart is presented in the table on page 28.[20]

To apply the basic strategy table, locate your two-card hand in the leftmost column, then move across to the entry corresponding to the dealer's upcard. For example, if you're dealt ace,7 (soft 18) and the dealer has a 5 as his upcard, you should double down if possible; otherwise you should stand.

---

[20] Experienced readers will note that our generic basic strategy is most appropriate for games in which doubling down is not allowed after splitting (noDAS). However, we advocate the generic basic strategy regardless of whether or not doubling after splitting is allowed. The loss in expectation from using the noDAS strategy in a DAS game is only 0.01%, and in our opinion does not justify its memorization.

GENERIC BASIC STRATEGY CHART

Dealer's Upcard

Player's Hand	2	3	4	5	6	7	8	9	10	A
A-A	Sp	Sp	Sp	Sp	Sp	Sp	Sp	Sp	Sp	Sp
10-10	S	S	S	S	S	S	S	S	S	S
9-9	Sp	Sp	Sp	Sp	Sp	S	Sp	Sp	S	S
8-8	Sp	Sp	Sp	Sp	Sp	Sp	Sp	Sp	Sp	Sp
7-7	Sp	Sp	Sp	Sp	Sp	Sp	H	H	H	H
6-6	H	Sp	Sp	Sp	Sp	H	H	H	H	H
5-5	D	D	D	D	D	D	D	D	H	H
4-4	H	H	H	H	H	H	H	H	H	H
3-3	H	H	Sp	Sp	Sp	Sp	H	H	H	H
2-2	H	H	Sp	Sp	Sp	Sp	H	H	H	H
Hard 17 ↑	S	S	S	S	S	S	S	S	S	S
Hard 16	S	S	S	S	S	H	H	Su/H	Su/H	Su/H
Hard 15	S	S	S	S	S	H	H	H	Su/H	H
Hard 14	S	S	S	S	S	H	H	H	H	H
Hard 13	S	S	S	S	S	H	H	H	H	H
Hard 12	H	H	S	S	S	H	H	H	H	H
11	D/H	D/H	D/H	D/H	D/H	D/H	D/H	D/H	D/H	H
10	D/H	D/H	D/H	D/H	D/H	D/H	D/H	D/H	H	H
9	H	D/H	D/H	D/H	D/H	H	H	H	H	H
8 ↓	H	H	H	H	H	H	H	H	H	H
Soft 19 ↑	S	S	S	S	S	S	S	S	S	S
Soft 18	S	D/S	D/S	D/S	D/S	S	S	H	H	H
Soft 17	H	D/H	D/H	D/H	D/H	H	H	H	H	H
Soft 16	H	H	D/H	D/H	D/H	H	H	H	H	H
Soft 15	H	H	D/H	D/H	D/H	H	H	H	H	H
Soft 14	H	H	H	D/H	D/H	H	H	H	H	H
Soft 13	H	H	H	D/H	D/H	H	H	H	H	H

NEVER TAKE INSURANCE

KEY:

S=Stand   H=Hit   D=Double Down   Sp=Split   Su=Surrender

x/y=Do x if possible, otherwise do y   *see pg. 147 for early surrender*

GENERIC BASIC STRATEGY RULES

Never take **insurance.**

For **splitting pairs**:
* Always split a pair of aces or 8s.
* Never split a pair of tens, 5s, or 4s.
* Split 9s against a dealer's 9 or less, except 7.
* Split 7s against a dealer's 7 or less.
* Split 6s against a dealer's 6 or less, except 2.
* Split 2s and 3s against a dealer's 4 through 7.

For **doubling down (DD)**:
* With soft 17 or 18, DD against a dealer's 3 through 6.
* With soft 15 or 16, DD against a dealer's 4 through 6.
* With soft 13 or 14, DD against a dealer's 5 and 6.
* With 10 or 11, DD if total is more than dealer's upcard.
* With 9, DD against a dealer's 3 through 6.
* Never DD with hard 8 or less.

For **hard hands**:
* With 17 or more, always stand.
* With 12 through 16, hit against a dealer's upcard of 7 or more, otherwise stand. (The only exception to this rule is to hit a hard 12 vs a dealer 2 or 3.)
* With 11 or less, always hit (unless doubling).

For **soft hands**:
* With soft 19 or more, always stand.
* With soft 18, hit against a dealer's 9 or more, otherwise stand (unless doubling).
* With soft 17 or less, always hit (unless doubling).

Alternatively, if you hold 7,7 and the dealer shows a 7 as his upcard, you should split the pair instead of hitting the 14.

The basic strategy should be memorized. This is not as daunting a feat as you might first think. In fact, if you're at least a casual player, you probably know most of it already.

There are several general patterns to observe that will aid in understanding and memorizing the basic strategy. First, most of the splitting occurs against weak dealer upcards. Aces and 8s are always split. The splitting of 8s is often a defensive play, since a poor hand of 16 is potentially converted into two reasonable hands. The splitting of aces is mostly offensive, as a mediocre hand is converted into two strong ones. Pairs of 4s,[21] 5s, or tens are never split; doing so would generally weaken the hand.

Of interest is the play with a pair of 9s. We go ahead and split them against a 6 or less. In this case, the split is an offensive maneuver as we're trying to kick the dealer when he's down. Against a 7, though, we stand; the chance of a dealer busting with a 7 up is much lower than with a 2 through 6 up (roughly 26% vs. 40%). Furthermore, the chance that a dealer will reach a total of exactly 17 rises dramatically (to 37%), hence there's a good chance that our 18 will win by the slimmest of margins. Against an 8, we split 9s in an offensive move. Splitting 9s against a 9 is an attempt to salvage a losing hand. Against a ten or ace, we take a deep breath and stand with our 18; there's not much else to do but wait for the likely coup de grace.

Doubling-down plays typically occur against a weak dealer upcard, where the introduction of an additional wager is most warranted. We generally double down if we expect to win the hand and expect to want only one hit.

Let's also look at the hitting and standing strategy rela-

---

[21] The rule to never split 4s assumes our generic basic strategy. In a DAS game, readers so inclined may additionally split a pair of 6s vs. a dealer 2, 4s vs. 5 or 6, and 2s and 3s vs. 2 or 3, the so-called DAS strategy.

tive to dealer's bust percentages by upcard. If you're holding a stiff hand (12-16), you generally hit against a strong dealer upcard, since he's likely to reach a pat total of 17 through 21. However, against a weak dealer upcard, you generally stand, forcing the dealer to draw with an increased frequency of busting. Again, a good mnemonic crutch (though not always true) when holding a stiff is to play your hand assuming the dealer has a ten in the hole—a reasonable rule of thumb given that there are four times as many tens as any other card in the pack.

JUDICIOUS BASIC STRATEGY PLAY

Some players have trouble adhering to the basic strategy. One rule in particular that many have a hard time understanding is the hitting of stiff hands. For many, it's particularly difficult to hit a hard 16. Since the player has such a great chance of busting, it's easy to balk at taking a hit, especially if the dealer has a 7 showing. The dealer's 7 is not that strong, they reason, so why risk busting. The ulterior motive, of course, is to last longer. "You stay, you play," right?

In fact, this strategy will cause them to play less overall because they increase their loss rate. It turns out that by standing with 16 vs. a 7, the player loses about 48¢ for every $1 wagered. On the other hand, by hitting, the loss is only 42¢. Now, a difference of 6¢ might not seem like much, but it adds up. With a $25 bet out, making the incorrect play in this situation will cost you an average of $1.50.

Looking at the choice in terms of win/loss/tie percentages (rather than dollar amounts), an analysis shows that players who stand will win only if the dealer busts, with probability 26%. By hitting, the chance of winning is increased to 27%, and there is roughly a 4% chance of pushing. Overall, it may seem like you have a better chance by standing with a 16 versus a 7, but most of the time you are gaining only a

BLACKJACK Fallacy

Ride the wave

A colleague visiting Foxwoods Casino one evening witnessed an interesting series of events. A young college student had been playing for the better part of two days. Shoe after shoe, the fellow would cash out a profit on the previous series of hands. As our colleague approached, the collegiate was "waiting to lose just one shoe" so he could go home. Poor guy.

The individual used a betting progression and made a rather erratic strategic play by doubling down on hard 12—always! While doubling hard 12 is a very poor play, he couldn't seem to lose and was already up several thousands of dollars.

Well, after watching the college fellow win over the course of several more shoes, our colleague decided to "press his luck" by backlining the player. (Backlining is a procedure allowed in some casinos by which you can wager along with the player making the original wager, abiding by the way he plays his hand.) The player kept doubling hard 12s, but also kept right on winning for the next few hours.

Even though our heroes were lucky this time around, the misplay of the 12 adversely affected their expected return. Apparent "hot" streaks are hard to resist, but there is no way of knowing if they are about to end or how long they will last.[22] There is no way to capitalize on them. In the long run, "hunch" players will always fare worse than players employing the correct strategy.

---

[22] See Olaf Vancura's *Smart Casino Gambling*, 1996, Index Publishing.

brief respite before your demise. Sometimes, as in this case, the correct basic strategy play is the lesser of two evils. It's not that playing correct basic strategy will turn bad hands into good ones; it's that proper basic strategy tends to minimize losses on those bad hands.

A similar line of reasoning can be applied to the other basic strategy plays. In the end, it's a comparison of expected value that determines the best option.

The basic strategy must be followed exactly. There's no room for superstition or hunches. In the example given earlier, even if you've hit 16 vs. 7 three times in a row and busted each time, you've got to do it again when presented with the same situation. On the other hand, if the last time you hit 16 vs. 7 you hooked a 5, you may feel inclined not to press your luck. Here again, though, you must; in the long run, it is the best mathematical play. Don't let your emotions be your guide; this is exactly what the casinos want.

A WORD ON INSURANCE

The basic strategy says to never take insurance. Don't even consider it. Despite what casinos would have you believe, insurance is a bet solely on whether or not the dealer has a natural. Since the ace is already showing, you're wagering on whether or not the downcard is a ten.

The insurance bet neither increases nor decreases your chances of winning the main bet. As such, taking insurance is strictly a side bet. Whether or not you win it, the main hand will be played to its completion. If the dealer has the natural, then insurance pays 2 to 1, but the main hand is lost (unless you, too, have a natural and push); if the dealer doesn't have the blackjack, the insurance bet is lost and the main hand is played out in the normal fashion. Either way, you can see that your insurance bet doesn't "buy" you anything on the

---

BLACKJACK Fallacy

Insure the good hands

Of course, casinos want players to make poor wagers. As such, insurance is promoted as a way to "guarantee" a good hand. But in reality, holding a good hand is often the worst time to take insurance.

For example, consider two possible scenarios for the first hand out of a shoe. In the first scenario you are dealt a 2,3 with a dealer ace showing. The second scenario has you holding a hand of J,Q vs. the same dealer upcard. Question: In which case should you take insurance? Answer: Neither, but you are more likely to win the insurance wager while holding the hand of 2,3. This is because in the other case you are already holding two ten-valued cards, so the chance that the dealer has a ten as the downcard is correspondingly smaller.

---

main hand.

We can easily estimate the disadvantage of taking insurance. With no knowledge of cards played, we can assume that the remaining cards are in roughly the same proportion as in the full pack. Thus, regardless of the number of decks in use, the chance of the downcard being a ten (10, jack, queen, or king) is roughly 4/13. On the other hand, the chance that the downcard is not a ten (ace through 9) is roughly 9/13. The expected outcome for each dollar wagered on insurance is then roughly:

$$Expected\ Outcome_{Insurance} = \frac{4}{13}(+2) + \frac{9}{13}(-1) = -\frac{1}{13}$$

Insure the "sure" winner

BLACKJACK
Fallacy

Taking insurance when holding a blackjack—the so-called "even-money" payoff—is also a poor play. Let's say you've made a $100 wager, are dealt a natural, and the dealer has an ace showing. If you take even money, you'll wind up $100 richer. On the other hand, if you insure the natural for $50, one of two things can happen: 1) the dealer has a natural, in which case the naturals push, but you win $100 on the insurance bet; 2) the dealer doesn't have a natural, in which case your natural wins $150, but you lose $50 on the insurance bet. In either case, you wind up $100 ahead. Many players who "never" take insurance do take even money, not realizing they are one and the same when holding a natural.

It sounds logical, since insuring a blackjack means that you can't lose. In fact, some dealers go so far as to say, "It's the one sure bet in the house." But the catch is you win less, on average, by doing so. The expected outcome for insuring a natural is to profit $1 for every $1 wagered on the main bet. But when we don't insure our natural, our expected outcome for each $1 wagered is to profit more than $1, roughly:

$$Expected\ Outcome = \frac{4}{13}(0) + \frac{9}{13}\left(+\frac{3}{2}\right) = +1\frac{1}{26}$$

An average return of 1 1/26 is clearly greater than a sure return of 1. Unless you need the money to buy baby a new pair of shoes (in which case you shouldn't have been betting anyway), it's best never to insure your natural if you are playing according to the basic strategy.

You can expect to lose 1/13 of every $1 wagered on insurance, corresponding to an expectation of nearly –7.7% (or a loss of 7.7¢ per $1). Without any other information about deck composition, insurance should *never* be taken.

BASIC STRATEGY STRENGTH

What can you expect (in terms of return percentages) when you play blackjack by the basic strategy? It depends on the game you're playing; the number of decks being dealt and the rules in force affect the expected return. For almost all games you encounter, the basic strategy player's expectation is between –0.7% and +0.1%. The majority will actually be between –0.6% and 0.0%.

We've generated the following table to guide you in estimating the approximate effects of rules variations on the basic strategy player. (The table was generated by simulation assuming our generic basic strategy and should be used only as a guide. The effects of rules variations often depend on the number of decks in play. We have assumed the average effect for the purposes of constructing the table on pg. 37.)

The benchmark is for the set of rules often referred to as the "Las Vegas Strip game." The top-of-the-deck expectation is effectively –0.02%, making it nearly an even game.[23]

To estimate the expectation for a particular game, we can, to a good approximation, start with the benchmark and adjust for any rules changes by simply adding their effects.

For a typical Atlantic City (or Foxwoods, Conn.) game, the difference from our benchmark is the use of 6 or 8 decks and the

---

[23] In fact, with a basic strategy specific to the single-deck game (as opposed to the generic strategy presented herein), the expectation rises slightly to 0.00%.

APPROXIMATE EFFECT OF RULES VARIATIONS ON GENERIC BASIC STRATEGY EXPECTATION

Benchmark*	−0.02%
One-half deck	+0.71%
Two decks	−0.32%
Four decks	−0.48%
Six decks	−0.53%
Eight decks	−0.55%
Dealer wins ties	−9.34%
Natural pays 1 to 1	−2.32%
Natural pays 2 to 1	+2.32%
Dealer hits soft 17	−0.20%
No resplitting of any pairs	−0.03%
Resplitting of aces	+0.06%
No soft doubling	−0.11%
Double down only on 10 or 11	−0.21%
Double down only on 11	−0.69%
Double down on any number of cards	+0.24%
Double down after pair splitting	+0.13%
Late surrender	+0.06%

*Single deck; double down on any first two cards only;
one card on split aces; dealer stands on soft 17; no surrender.*

---

allowance of doubling after splitting. Hence we can estimate our expectation for the 8-decker to be the following:

Benchmark	−0.02%
Eight decks	−0.55%
Double down after pair splitting	+0.13%
Approx. player expectation	−0.44%

For a downtown Reno game, typical rules are dealer hits soft 17 (the other dealer hit/stand rules remain the same) and players may double down only on two-card totals of 10 or 11. For a 2-deck Reno game, the expectation is significantly worse:

Benchmark game	–0.02%
Two decks	–0.32%
Dealer hits soft 17	–0.20%
Double down only on 10 or 11	<u>–0.21%</u>
Approx. player expectation	–0.75%

For a single-deck Reno game, the expectation is about –0.43%, in the ballpark of a multiple-deck shoe game on the East Coast or in Las Vegas. Trade-offs like this, where multiple-deck games have more liberal doubling and splitting rules (or alternatively, single-deck games impose restrictive doubling), are commonplace and can often be found within the same casino.

Rules variations from casino to casino can have a significant impact on your expectation, hence earnings. Independent of finding favorable card-counting conditions as described later in this book, we recommend always playing the best available game. Though this may require going to a different casino, often all that's needed is a short walk around the pit. It's not uncommon for a single casino to offer a range of games with basic strategy expectations that differ by 0.3% or more.

Before we take a look at some of the entries in the "Effect of Rules Variations" table, a few words on the effects of multiple decks are in order. Why, for the same basic strategy, does a multiple-deck game have a worse expectation than a single-deck game? Peter Griffin, in *The Theory of Blackjack*, gives three primary reasons: natural 21s occur less frequently in multiple-deck packs; doubling down is less advantageous in multiple-deck packs; and "judicious standing with stiff totals" is less advantageous.

I'm gonna stand on my ace,5

BLACKJACK
Fallacy

Some superstitious players refuse to hit hands such as soft 16, somehow believing their hand might be made worse by doing so. The fact is, anytime a player stands on 16 or less, the only chance of winning is if the dealer busts. So *all* hands of 16 or less are equivalent. If you've stood, a hard 16 has the same chance of winning as a soft 12 (two aces) or a total of 5 consisting of 2,3.

Never stand on any soft total of 16 or less. There is no penalty for taking another hit; your hand cannot get worse. Similarly, you should never stand on any total of 11 or less. Again, your hand cannot be made worse with another hit.

These consequences each occur because, as you might expect, the effect of removing individual cards is more pronounced in single-deck than in multiple-deck games. For example, when doubling with a hand of 7,3 against a dealer upcard of 4, the player is hoping to get either an ace or a ten. Considering the three cards in play, the player still has four aces and sixteen tens available. The chance of drawing one of them in a single-deck game is therefore 20/49 (or 0.408). In an 8-deck game, on the other hand, the chance would be considerably less at 160/413 (0.387), a success rate only 95% that of the single-deck game. You can see that the three cards already in play (in this example) improve the player's chances for success in the single-deck case.

Here's another example of this effect. Consider one of the key advantages afforded the player: the bonus paid on naturals. In an 8-deck game, the "off-the-top" chance of receiving a two-card total of 21 is 4.75%, while in a single deck it's 4.83%. Even more striking, assuming we have a natural in hand, the chance that the dealer also possesses one is a sensitive function of the number of decks in play. In an 8-deck game, the dealer's chance of duplicating our natural is 4.61%, while in a single deck, it drops precipitously to 3.67%.

Clearly, the more restrictive the doubling-down rules, the more the player is hurt—though not badly. It may seem that restricting doubling down to only 10 and 11 should "cost" us more than 0.21%. But in reality, most of the gain in doubling down comes from these two plays. In addition, it may seem that allowing double downs on any number of cards should be worth more than 0.24%. However, on soft hands, the double has usually occurred (if at all) on the initial two cards. Furthermore, being dealt a three-card total of 10 or 11 happens very infrequently.

A game where the dealer wins all ties is catastrophic to a player's profitability. Even card counters will be unable to beat this game. Charity-night blackjack games often incorporate this "feature" to ensure that the house makes money during the event.

A SIMPLIFIED BASIC STRATEGY

For those new to the game, the basic strategy as presented may seem a bit intimidating. As such, we've boiled down the rules to a simplified set for novices. While the simplified set is sufficient for casual play, the simplification *does* come at the expense of power. For a typical game, using the simplified basic strategy costs you an extra 0.35%, compared to our generic basic strategy expectation. Thus, in a benchmark 6-deck game, your expectation would be roughly –0.90%, still

---

SIMPLIFIED BASIC STRATEGY RULES

Never take **insurance.**

For **splitting pairs:**
• Always split a pair of aces or 8s.

For **doubling down:**
• With 10 or 11, double down if your total is greater than the dealer's upcard.

For **hard hands:**
• With 17 or more, always stand.
• With 12 through 16, hit against a dealer's upcard of 7 or more, otherwise stand.
• With 11 or less, always hit (unless doubling).

For **soft hands:**
• With soft 18 or more, always stand.
• With soft 17 or less, always hit.

---

an expected payback in excess of 99%, which is better than almost any other game you can play in a casino.

SUMMARY

• Basic strategy is a set of playing rules based on the cards in your hand and the dealer's upcard.

• Deviation from the basic strategy, without any other information about deck composition, will cost you in the long run.

• In principle, the basic strategy matrix is slightly different for different playing conditions. However, the differences are subtle and minor. The change in expectation between applying our generic basic strategy table and the appropriate exact table, which is a function of the number of decks and rules in force, is typically 0.03% or less, and therefore, not worth the effort to remember.

A WORD ON NOTATION

From this point forward, we will periodically refer to certain rules in their abbreviated notation. For example, the rule "Double Down on any first two cards" is abbreviated to **DOA**, which stands for "Double On Anything." Another common rule variation concerns the dealer's hitting/standing on soft 17. If the dealer stands on soft 17, we refer to this as **S17**. On the other hand, games in which the dealer hits soft 17 are abbreviated **H17**. If doubling down is allowed after splitting, we call this **DAS**. If not, the game is **noDAS**.

Round 3

An Introduction to Card Counting

Chance favors the prepared mind.
—Louis Pasteur

You may be wondering what makes blackjack different from other gambling games. Why is it that a skilled player can beat blackjack, but has no hope of ever beating a game like craps over the long term? It boils down to the mathematical concept of independent and dependent trials.

In games like craps, roulette, slot machines, big six, Let It Ride, and Caribbean Stud, each and every round is independent from all other rounds. Even if a shooter has thrown a natural on four straight crap hands, the chances of success or failure on the next hand do not change. In fact, there is no information whatsoever to be gained by studying the outcome of previous trials.[24] There is no point

---

[24] The statement is strictly true for fair equipment played in a fair manner. See Vancura's *Smart Casino Gambling* for a discussion of some novel attempts to beat faulty casino roulette or state lottery equipment.

in trying to jump in on "hot" streaks and exit early on "cold" streaks; there is no predictive ability.

In blackjack, successive hands are *dependent* events. This means that past events can and do influence what happens in the future. Specifically, the cards already played affect the composition of the remaining deck, which in turn affects your future chances of winning.

Consider a single-deck blackjack game. If, in the first round after a shuffle, player one is dealt a pair of aces, while players two and three each receive naturals, then we have useful information about what may take place in the future. First, we know that no naturals can appear in the second round. Why? Because all four aces have already appeared in round one. In this instance, the players are at a severe disadvantage (and the house is at a correspondingly high advantage). Card counting identifies those times when the deck composition favors the player, allowing us to bet more when we have the advantage.

We note that baccarat, like blackjack, is a game of dependent events. However, in the case of baccarat, only a tiny advantage can be gained through the tracking of cards. This comes about because the banker and player draw to very similar fixed sets of rules, the result being that no card strongly favors either the player or the dealer.[25]

In Chapter 2 we learned that by finding a good blackjack game and playing basic strategy, we can chop the house advantage down to between 0% and 0.5%. Keeping track of the cards (counting) will allow us to push over the top to secure an advantage.

---

[25] For a further discussion of baccarat, see Thorp's *The Mathematics of Gambling*, Griffin's *The Theory of Blackjack*, or Vancura's *Smart Casino Gambling*.

COUNTING GUMBALLS

To illustrate the concept of dependent trials, let's take a step back into our childhood.

You're at the local grocery store, and standing before you is a gumball machine filled with exactly 10 white and 10 black gumballs. You know this because you saw the store manager refill it just five minutes ago. All the balls are thoroughly mixed together, and there's a line of kids waiting to purchase them.

Your friend, being the betting type and needing only a couple more dollars to buy that model airplane he's been eyeing, makes the following proposition. You are allowed to bet $1 (let's pretend we're rich kids) whenever you wish that the next ball to come out will be white. If a white ball comes out, you win $1. If a black ball comes out, you lose $1. Sounds like a simple enough game, you say to yourself.

If you bet right off the top, there are a total of 20 gumballs, of which 10 will win for you. Your chance of winning is thus 10/20, or simply 1/2. Not surprisingly, your chance of losing is also 1/2. So your expected outcome is simply:

$$Expected\ Outcome = \frac{1}{2}(+1) + \frac{1}{2}(-1) = 0$$

The expected outcome of 0 implies that, over the long run, you are expected to neither win nor lose money if you bet on the very first ball. Of course, each individual wager will result in either a $1 win or a $1 loss, but over time your *expectation* is to net 0 on this 50/50 proposition.

Let's say, however, that one gumball has already come out, and you know that it was white.

Since there are now 10 black balls (losers) and only 9 white balls (winners) left, making the bet would place you at a disadvantage. Your chance of winning is 9/19, but your chance of losing is 10/19. The expected outcome has become:

$$Expected\ Outcome\ = \frac{4}{9}(+1) + \frac{5}{9}(-1) = -\frac{1}{9}$$

For every $1 you wager on white at this point, you expect to lose 1/19 of $1, or a little more than 5¢. That is, in the long run your expectation is to lose 5.26% of your wager. Again, each individual wager will result in either a $1 win or a $1 loss, but over the long haul you will lose more often than win, which leads to your demise at an average rate of 5¢ per play.

Now consider a situation where there are 10 white and 9 black gumballs left. In this case, you have the advantage, and it's times like these that you will go ahead and make the bet. Following the above example, it's easy to see that the expectation is +5.26%. Every bet you make in this situation is a long-run moneymaker.

Clearly, if your intention is to play this game for profit, you should play only when you have a positive expectation, and never play when the expectation is negative. So the question is: How can you identify the times when making the bet is favorable?

A simple way to determine whether or not you have the advantage is to track the gumballs so you have information about how many of each color remain in the dispenser. We know that removing black gumballs from the machine helps you: Every time a black ball is taken out of play, your expectation (for betting on white) goes up slightly. The opposite is true when a white gumball is removed. So to begin, we can assign black balls a value of +1 and white balls a value of −1 (these assignments are sometimes referred to as "tags").

Start at zero and keep a "running count" of all the balls as they come out of the machine. After a ball is seen, the running count is updated by adding its value. For example, if the first ball to come out is black, then the running count is +1. If the next ball is white, the running count goes back to 0 (arrived at by starting with +1 for the old running count and adding –1 for the white ball that just came out).

As you may have deduced, the running count alerts you to when it's profitable to play—whenever the running count is positive, you have the advantage. You don't need to count (and remember) the exact number of white and black balls played; you don't even need to know how many balls are left. You need only know the value of the running count to know whether or not you have an edge. The point at which we know you first have the advantage is called the "key count." At or above the key count (+1), you have the advantage; below the key count, you are either neutral or at a disadvantage.

Note that gumballs of other colors (that don't win or lose our wager) can be introduced without affecting our ability to maintain the count. We simply ignore them. For example, adding 10 red balls, 13 blue balls, and 5 green balls does not make our counting any more difficult. We simply assign a value of 0 to each of these extra colors, which do not change the running count as they exit.

This is the basic concept behind card counting—employing a weighting system to determine who, player or casino, has the advantage.

PIVOTS AND IRCS

There are many differences between blackjack and gumballs, but let's stay with our gumball example a little longer to demonstrate two additional concepts: the "pivot" and the "IRC."

Though ultra-simple, the gumball count system has a fairly serious drawback. While we always know *when* we have an advantage, we often have little information about how great (or small) it is. For example, a running count equal to the key count of +1 could occur with 1 white and 0 black balls remaining (an expectation of +100%), or with 10 white and 9 black balls left (an expectation of "only" +5.26%).[26]

Indeed, for the game starting with 10 white and 10 black gumballs, the only time we have a precise handle on the expectation is when the running count is exactly 0. At this point, we know our expectation is precisely 0%.[27] We may therefore define the pivot point as the count at which we have reliable information about our expectation. The pivot point is important because, later, we will base betting strategies on this gauge of our expectation.

To further illustrate this effect, let's alter the initial conditions. Instead of 10 white and 10 black, let's assume that there are initially 20 white, 24 black, and 8 yellow gumballs. We can still use our counting system (black = +1, white = −1, yellow = 0) to track the game. But if we start at a count of zero, we no longer have the advantage when the count is just slightly greater than zero. It's easy to see why. If a black ball comes out, our count is +1. However, we are still at a disadvantage in the game since 23 losing black balls remain, compared to only 20 winning white balls (remember, the 8 yellow balls don't matter).

A little thought will convince you that in this case, with a starting count of zero, we always have an expectation of 0 when the running count is +4 (indicating that the number of white and black balls remaining is equal). Hence, the pivot point for this game is +4. Further reflection will reveal that we now need the running count to be equal to or greater than +5 to have the advantage. The key count for this game is

---

[26] The way out of this problem is to keep a separate count of the total balls remaining. In this case, dividing the running count by the number of balls remaining gives the exact value for the expectation.

[27] This effect and nomenclature was first introduced by Arnold Snyder.

therefore +5. As you can see, both the key count and the pivot point changed in response to altered starting conditions.

Since this can all become a bit unwieldy, we can, if we choose, make an adjustment in the point at which we begin our count. That is, we adjust the "initial running count" (IRC) in order to provide more convenient key-count and pivot-point numbers. For example, we could start the IRC at, say, +2, and then we'd have the advantage when the running count was equal to or greater than +7. Or we could use an IRC of –4, in which case we'd have the advantage when the count was equal to or greater than +1.

The point of all this is that the pivot point and key count are a function of what we choose as the IRC. We'll see later how this can be used to simplify our system.

Let's review.

• To get an advantage in our gumball game, we can assign an integer value to each colored gumball and keep a running count of those we've seen come out of the machine.

• Two special count values are the key count, at or above which we have the advantage, and the pivot point, at which we have reliable information about our expectation.

• The key count and pivot point will depend on our initial running count.

Counting cards is not dissimilar to counting gumballs. First, just as there were good gumballs, bad gumballs, and neutral gumballs, in blackjack there are good cards, bad cards, and neutral cards. And just as we assigned a value to the different gumballs, we can also assign a value to each type of card. We then start with an initial running count and count through the deck as the cards are played. Once the running count reaches the key count, we know we generally have the advantage. When the running count is equal to the pivot point, we have a reliable estimate of the expectation.

ALL CARDS ARE NOT CREATED EQUAL

Okay, we know that keeping track of cards already played tells us about hands yet to come. But to make use of this information, we need to know which cards are beneficial to us as players, and which cards are not. Once we know this, tracking the cards played will tell us when the remaining deck is to our liking. Ultimately, we will bet small when the remaining deck is unsavory, and bet big when it's juicy. Anyone hungry yet?

To help determine which cards are good for us and which are bad, we must consider the rules of the game and the difference in playing strategies between a basic strategy player and a dealer employing the house rules. A lot can be gleaned from this comparison; there are several factors at work that show why it's important to be able to distinguish between decks made up of predominantly high cards and decks made up of predominantly low cards:

1. The payoff structure for naturals favors the player.

When the remaining deck has an excess of aces and tens, you're more likely to be dealt a natural. This fact favors the player. Although the dealer is always as likely as we are to receive a blackjack, our two-card 21 is paid at a premium. Imagine a game in which there is at least one natural guaranteed to show each hand; that is, on each deal the player and/ or dealer will have a blackjack. Let's suppose we are betting $20 a hand. When we and the dealer get a blackjack, we push and no money changes hands. When the dealer has a natural and we don't, we lose $20. But when we have a natural and the dealer doesn't, we win $30 because our blackjack pays 3 to 2. We come out far ahead overall.

2. The dealer must hit until reaching a pat total of 17 through 21.

All casino dealers play by a fixed set of rules: any hand of 16 or less must be hit and, of course, any hand of 22 or more is busted. Totals of 17, 18, 19, 20, and 21 can be thought of as a "safe zone" into which the dealer climbs, then stops. Clearly, with an excess of high cards remaining, the dealer's chances of reaching the safe zone, without going beyond it, when drawing to a stiff total decrease. On the other hand, if a lot of small cards remain, the dealer is more likely to draw to a pat hand. When an excess of big cards remains, the knowledgeable player can choose to stand on a stiff hand, forcing the dealer to draw from a deck rich with high cards and (hopefully) bust.

3. When doubling down, the player is usually hoping to get a high card.

Two conditions must generally exist for us to double down: (a) we expect to win the hand; (b) we are satisfied drawing only one more card. Furthermore, as noted in our discussion of the basic strategy, most double downs occur against a weak dealer upcard (a 3, 4, 5, or 6). An abundance of high-valued cards helps us in two ways here. Our hand is likely to improve greatly (if doubling on a total of 10 or 11), and the dealer is more likely to bust, especially when showing a weak upcard.

4. Many splitting opportunities are more favorable with an abundance of big cards left in the deck.

A look at the basic strategy table, and at the splitting discussion in Chapter 2, shows that a preponderance of high cards is usually beneficial to us when splitting, regardless of whether we are splitting offensively or defensively. This is especially true of splitting 7s, 8s, 9s, and aces.

5. Insurance can become a profitable bet.

This should not be underestimated, as the proper use of the insurance wager while card counting is worth roughly 0.15% (or more). As discussed in the basic strategy, we should never take insurance with no knowledge of deck composition. But if we're tracking the game and know that the ratio of tens to non-tens is large (greater than 1/2), then insurance should be taken. The great thing about insurance is that you take it only when you want to—it's an optional side bet that can be put to good use by a card counter.

These are the main reasons why certain card denominations are favorable or unfavorable for the player. Clearly, a deck relatively rich in high cards (or, equivalently, poor in low cards) is good for the player. Conversely, a deck rich in low cards (poor in high cards) favors the dealer.

ASSIGNING THE VALUES

To take the value of a card-counting system further, we need to know exactly how much each card is worth. To determine this, we simulate a benchmark single-deck game using the basic strategy. As mentioned in Chapter 2, we come up with an expectation of –0.02%.

We then simulate the same basic strategy in a single-deck game that has one card removed, for example a 2, and note the resulting expectation of +0.38%. Comparing the expectation of the two games gives us a measure of how valuable the 2 is. For this particular example, we find that removing the 2 is "worth" 0.40% to us.

We then repeat the process for each other card rank. In so doing, we can construct a table of the relative values of each card. (All values are changes in the expectation for the benchmark single-deck blackjack game, assuming we are playing by the fixed generic basic strategy of Chapter 2.[28])

---

[28] These values were derived from simulations of the benchmark game assuming a fixed generic basic strategy. In fact, the relative value of the cards is a slowly varying function of the game conditions and strategy adopted. See, e.g., Griffin's *The Theory of Blackjack* for values associated with the dealer's hitting soft 17.

The table below gives the change in player's expectation that arises from *removing* a card of a certain denomination. For example, if we remove just one 5 from a single deck, the change in player's expectation is +0.67%. For our benchmark single-deck game (with an initial expectation of –0.02%), the "new" expectation, after removing the 5, is now +0.65%. On the other hand, removing a single ace changes the expectation by –0.59%.

What happens if, for example, both an ace and a 5 are removed? To a very good approximation, we simply add the resulting effects. So the total change in expectation is –0.59% (for the ace) + 0.67% (for the 5) for a total change of +0.08%. Thus removing these two cards leaves us almost where we started; they've nearly canceled each other out. Refer to Fig-

RELATIVE VALUE OF CARDS IN SINGLE-DECK BLACKJACK ASSUMING A FIXED GENERIC BASIC STRATEGY

Removed Card	Change in Player's Expectation
2	+0.40%
3	+0.43%
4	+0.52%
5	+0.67%
6	+0.45%
7	+0.30%
8	+0.01%
9	–0.15%
ten	–0.51%
ace	–0.59%

ure 3 to see the cumulative effect of adding or removing aces and 5s (aces and 5s were chosen because these are the two cards that create the greatest change in expectation with their addition or removal).

As we've discussed, a deficit of high-valued cards, mainly aces and tens, is bad for the player. This is confirmed in the table below, where it can be seen that removing these cards from play (hence, creating a deficit of them) causes our expectation to go down. As players, we want the pack to contain an excess of these high-valued cards. We will label tens

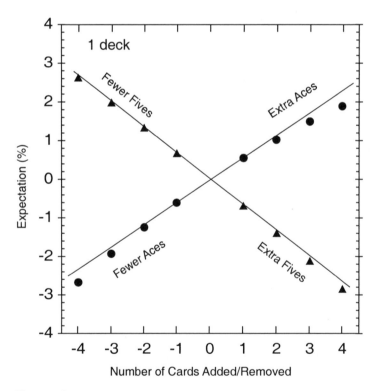

Figure 3: *The effects of adding/removing aces/5s, which are the two most "valuable" cards. Removing or adding additional like-cards leaves us with a change in expectation which nearly follows a straight line.*

and aces as *good cards*.

In this same vein, removing low cards (namely 2s through 7s) from the deck increases our expectation. In removing these cards, we are in effect creating an excess of high-valued cards, which gives us an advantage. These are the cards we'd like to see out of the deck. We will label 2s through 7s as *bad cards*.

We can now summarize the crux of card counting. We keep track of cards played in order to ascertain which cards remain unplayed. As the deck composition changes, the excess or deficit of good and bad cards shifts the advantage back and forth between the player and the house. The key, then, is to identify when we have the advantage and when we don't. We make big bets when we do and small bets when we don't. In so doing, the gains from the big bets will more than make up for the losses from the small bets. We will come out ahead in the long run.

COUNTING CARDS—THE OLD WAY

You should by now be ready to move on to the Knock-Out system. Before doing so, however, we'll take this opportunity to show you why we developed K-O. It's a matter of manageability: The traditional systems are just too difficult to implement. (For more on traditional vs. unbalanced, see Appendix 7.)

The example that follows is representative of the process a card counter using a traditional balanced count system must go through. Note that it's not necessary that you understand all of the steps, but we're sure that you'll appreciate the ease of K-O once you're aware of them.

Like all card-counting systems, balanced counts assign a value to each card (+1, −1, etc.). A running count is kept and continually updated.

THE CUT-CARD EFFECT

The "cut-card effect" is a subtle nuance that generally causes basic strategy to have a slightly worse expectation than the figure calculated "theoretically" off the top of the deck.[29] It generally has the greatest effect in a single-deck game.

The effect arises as follows. Let's say the cut card is placed about two-thirds of the way through the deck, at 36 cards. At an average of about 3 cards per hand and a total of 5-6 hands per round (4 or 5 players plus a dealer), roughly 36 cards are typically dealt out after two rounds.

However, if fewer cards have been dealt out and the dealer has not reached the cut card, another round will be dealt. What are the circumstances under which fewer cards will be dealt? Typically, it's a succession of hands in which a lot of high cards appear. This causes the average number of cards-per-hand to be less than three. So, the dealer preferentially deals out an extra round when the high cards have already been played!

Similarly, if a lot of low cards come out in the first two rounds, the dealer will assuredly reach the cut card at some point during the second round. Con-

---

[29] The cut-card effect has not been mathematically *proven* to exist, although it is plausible that the effect is real (Edward O. Thorp, private comm.; see also Thorp's revealing article "Does Basic Strategy Have the Same Expectation for Each Round?" in *Blackjack Forum*, June 1993). Simulations also demonstrate the effect, even in head-to-head play. For example, in a single-deck game with 65% penetration in which the dealer hits soft 17, our simulations suggest that the generic basic strategy player has an expectation of roughly -0.38%, as opposed to the "fixed number of rounds" value of 0.22% as depicted in Chapter 2.

sequently, there will be no third round of hands. The fact that the running count will be high (due to the excess of high cards now remaining) is immaterial, since the dealer will shuffle away the advantage.

Some casinos have gone so far as to introduce tables with only five betting spots to take advantage of this cut-card effect at their single-deck tables. And you thought they were just trying to give you more elbow room!

Now imagine the following 2-deck scenario. You're keeping the running count in your head; say it's +3. It's time to bet and the dealer is waiting on you. But before you can bet, the system requires that you convert the running count to a standardized measure, which is called a true count. Here's how it goes. While remembering the running count, you need to look over at the discard rack and estimate the number of decks already played—let's say a deck and a quarter. Now you think to yourself, "2 (decks) less 1 1/4 leaves 3/4 unplayed." Okay, now divide the running count (Still remember it? It's +3.) by the number of decks unplayed, and round down toward zero to get the true count. Quick, what's the answer? (It's 4.) Finally, you size your bet according to the true count of +4 and make the bet. It's necessary to repeat this process before you make every big wager.

Now that the wager is made, you have to go back to the running count (Still got it?) and count the cards as they're dealt. When it's your turn to play (dealer waiting on you again), it's often necessary to go through the process of converting to the true count again to decide how to play your cards. This constant conversion between running count and true count is mentally taxing, prone to error, and leads to quick fatigue. It certainly detracts from enjoyment of the game.

What's more, the mental gymnastics necessary to effect the true-count conversion are only part of the problem. Some systems are far more difficult due to demands such as the following:

Multiple-level card values—Many systems count by more than one numeral, incorporating higher-level values, for example –3 to +3. They're called "multi-level" counts. If you think counting up and down by 1 is tough, try counting up and down by 2, 3, or even 4 at a time.

Side counts—As if multiple levels and true-count conversions weren't enough, some systems would have you keep an extra count of certain cards, usually aces. These are called "multi-parameter" counts. Imagine keeping two separate running counts going in your head. Every time you see a 2 through king, you add its value to one running count, and every time you see an ace, you add to a different running count. When it's time to bet (or play), you need to compare the number of aces played with the average number that should have appeared at this point in the deck, estimate the discrepancy, then add to (or subtract from) the running count, prior to calculating the conversion to…Well, you get the picture.

Strategy-variation indices—Some systems require that you refer to complicated strategy-index matrices. These sometimes have upwards of 200 entries that need to be memorized in order to realize a small gain in performance.

This example may make you want to stop before you even step into the ring. Take heart; it's time to lighten up. The

Knock-Out system eliminates many of these steps, at virtually no reduction in power.

SUMMARY

• In blackjack, each hand is not an independent event, so the tracking of cards already played yields information on remaining deck content. The idea is to monitor the deck to determine when it's good or bad for the player. It's important to understand that card counters do not memorize every card that's played; they merely keep track of the relative number of high cards compared to low cards left in the deck. This can be done by assigning a value to each type of card and maintaining a running count of all cards seen. The player can then modify his betting and playing strategy accordingly.

• Certain deck compositions are favorable to the player, while others help the dealer. In particular, a deck that is rich in tens and aces favors the player. This is true for several reasons, among them the fact that blackjacks (which pay a bonus to the player) are more prevalent; the dealer is more likely to bust with a stiff; double down and split plays are more advantageous; and the insurance side bet can become profitable. On the other hand, a deck that is rich in low cards (or poor in tens and aces) favors the dealer.

• With regard to betting, when the deck is favorable the card counter will bet a lot. Conversely, when the deck is unfavorable, the card counter will bet a little or perhaps not play at all.

• While accurate and powerful, traditional balanced card-counting techniques that require a true-count conversion are often difficult to employ without error.

Round 4

The Unbalanced Knock-Out System

Everything should be as simple as possible, but not more so.
—Albert Einstein

Today's modern point-count systems are commonly classified according to three main categories: their level, type, and whether or not a side count is required. We touched on these at the end of Chapter 3. Let's take another look at each.

CLASSIFICATIONS

Level—Level refers to the integer values assigned to the cards themselves. If each card is assigned integer values of either -1, 0, or $+1$, this is said to be a level-1 count. Similarly, systems employing values between -2 and $+2$ are level-2 counts, and so forth. As a rule, it's easier to use a level-1 system than a higher-level system. This is partly because it's always easier to add and subtract 1 than to add 2 and subtract 3, etc. In addition, the expert card counter looks for card patterns that cancel to zero, which are more common in a level-1 count.

Type—Type refers to whether the card-counting system is balanced or unbalanced. Both balanced and unbalanced systems keep track of a running count (as introduced in Chapter 3), which is an up-to-date cumulative total of all cards already seen. Historically, balanced counts have been more popular and well-studied, because they provide more accurate playing strategies. But balanced counts require additional effort to employ, particularly during the true count conversion.

Even with perfect mental arithmetic, true-count conversion is a source of error, because players must *estimate* the number of decks remaining to be played. This is typically approximated to the nearest one-half deck, and often leads to a true-count conversion that may be off by about 10%. The use of an unbalanced count eliminates the need for a true-count conversion.

Side Count—Several balanced counts use an additional side count to enhance their power. These are often called "multi-parameter systems." Particularly because of the uniqueness of the ace, many systems assign it a neutral value in the point count, then count it separately (an "ace side count"). As you can imagine, keeping a separate count of aces (or any other card for that matter) greatly complicates the picture. Instead of keeping one count in your head, you now have to keep two of them. Needless to say, keeping side counts is mentally taxing. Quite often, chips, feet, cigarettes, drinks, or anything else that's handy are employed to facilitate the task.

Thankfully, we can avoid the worst of these headaches by using the K-O system. The K-O is a single-level single-parameter count. More important, though, is that K-O is unbalanced, which completely eliminates the necessity to convert to a true count. As you'll see later, K-O also eliminates, or greatly simplifies, most other tasks associated with successful card counting.

Let's get to the business at hand.

LEARNING THE K-O CARD-COUNTING VALUES

The first step in any card-counting system is assigning values to the respective cards. The unbalanced Knock-Out system employs the following card-counting values:

Card	K-O Value
KNOCK-OUT SYSTEM CARD-COUNTING VALUES	
Card	K-O Value
2	+1
3	+1
4	+1
5	+1
6	+1
7	+1
8	0
9	0
10, jack, queen, king	−1
ace	−1

The astute reader will immediately notice that there are more "+" than "−" designations. That's because the sum of the card tags does not equal zero. And that's why the K-O system is referred to as unbalanced.

Since the count values are restricted to +1, 0, or –1, and each card has only one value associated with it, the K-O system is a true level-1 system. A level-1 system allows for fast counting of a blackjack table full of cards. Combinations of cards that cancel to zero are easy to spot and eliminate from consideration. The suits of the cards are not considered, so a mere glance at a card is sufficient to determine its card-counting value.

To become a proficient card counter, you need to memorize the Knock-Out values of each card. In game conditions, you must be able to recall each Knock-Out value instantly.

LEARNING TO KEEP THE K-O RUNNING COUNT

To maintain the running count (or "RC"), we continually update it according to the cards that we see played. Based on the previous table, we add 1 for each low card (2, 3, 4, 5, 6, or 7), and subtract 1 for each high card (10, jack, queen, king, or ace) that we see. The RC is the important count that we need to remember, even during and in-between hands, and keep updating until the next shuffle.

The running count begins at the IRC. For reasons that will become clear in a moment, after a shuffle, we start with a *standard* initial running count that conforms with the following equation: 4 – (4 × *number of decks*). We adopt the term "standard" here as a reference point for discussion; later we will discuss ways to customize the K-O system (for example, to avoid the use of negative numbers).

Applying our equation, we start with a standard IRC of 0 for a single-deck game, IRC = 4 – (4 × 1 deck). For a double deck, it's 4 – (4 × 2) for an IRC of –4. For a 6-deck shoe, 4 – (4 × 6) equals a standard IRC of –20. The lowest standard IRC you will begin with is –28 for an 8-deck shoe game.

By starting with an IRC equal to 4 – (4 5 number of decks), we will always end with a count of +4 after all the cards in a pack have been counted. Because of the unbalanced point

---

DEALING WITH NEGATIVE NUMBERS

Dealing with negative numbers is nothing to be alarmed about.[30] Just imagine a number line with zero in the middle, positive numbers increase to the right and negative numbers increase in magnitude to the left.

To refresh the memories of those who may not have recently been exposed to negatives, adding a positive number means we move to the right on the number line. On the other hand, adding a negative number (or equivalently subtracting a positive number) means we move to the left.

-5 -4 -3 -2 -1 0 1 2 3 4 5

For example, if we're at a total of −4 and we want to add 1, we move to the right and arrive at a new total of −3. That is, (−4) + (1) = −3. Or, if we're at 1 and subtract 2, then the sum is −1. In other words, (1) − (2) = −1, which is the same as (1) + (−2). When you visualize the number system in this left-right fashion, it becomes fairly easy to do the necessary addition and subtraction.

---

[30] As mentioned, for those with an aversion to negative numbers, we'll later discuss alternatives to the standard K-O counting scheme.

values, each deck has a net count of +4, so the net count of the entire pack will exactly cancel out the "4 × *number of decks*" initially subtracted and leave us with +4 as the sum.

Let's look at a 2-deck game as an example. The IRC for a double decker is 4 – (4 × 2) = –4. As we count through the deck, the running count will generally rise from the IRC of –4 toward the final count, which will be +4 after all cards are counted. In practice, the running count will jump around on its journey, sometimes dipping downward below –4 and at other times cresting above +4. But at the end, it must equal +4 if we've counted correctly.

Figure 4 shows what a *representative* running count distribution might look like in the 2-deck game. We'll soon see that these statistical variations are what we, as counters, will take advantage of while playing.

The *average* running count behaves quite differently. In this case, the assumption is that we've played a great many hands, rendering the statistical variations negligible. On average, we expect the running count to rise linearly with the number of decks (total cards) already played, such that the rate of increase is +4 per deck.

FOUR STEPS TO KEEPING THE K-O RUNNING COUNT

To achieve proficiency at maintaining the running count, we recommend the following steps.

1. Memorize the Knock-Out card-counting value associated with each card.

Your recognition of the values of the card tags should be as natural as telling time. It should become ingrained and second nature.

One former professional card counter, a colleague of the

author Lawrence Revere some 20 years ago, described it like this: "To this day I can't get away from card-counting values. When I turn on my computer and it says 'Windows 95,' I see the 9 and 5 and still automatically think +2." (The system he uses is not K-O, and values 5s as +2 and 9s as 0.)

Similarly, you should be able to recall the card-counting values without pausing. It's important that this step be instantaneous. You should be able to look at a card and instantly recall its value of +1, 0, or –1 without hesitation.

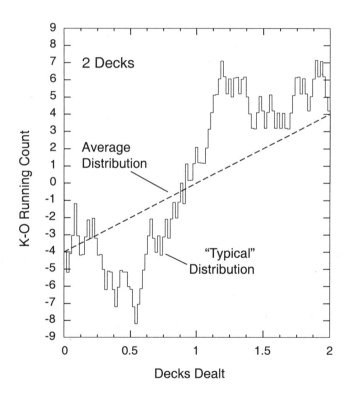

Figure 4: *A representative journey of the standard running count in a 2-deck game, with the running count plotted vs. the number of cards already played. The depiction is representative only in the sense that it gives a flavor of the magnitude of fluctuations during the course of play. Note the contrast with the average running count, represented by the ascending straight line.*

BLACKJACK Fallacy

Pictures follow pictures

Players who have just seen a face card come out will often refuse to hit their own stiff hands, believing that "pictures always follow pictures." Clearly, a face card can't always follow another face card (what if it was the last one?). In fact, it turns out that given that a picture card has just appeared, the chances of the next one also being a picture actually decrease.

This can be likened to a gumball machine where a known number of yellow gumballs (representing the picture cards) and green gumballs (representing the other cards) have been mixed together. Let's say we buy a gumball and it's yellow. The chance that the next one is also yellow has clearly decreased, since we've already taken one of the yellows out.

Similarly, all else being equal, given that the last card was a picture, it is less likely that the next card will be another picture card.

Begin with a deck of shuffled cards. As you turn each card over, recall its Knock-Out value. (Note: You don't want to recite it aloud, as this could lead to the troublesome habit of mouthing the count.) For example, for a sequence of cards 3, 5, king, 2, 8, queen, you would silently think +1, +1, −1, +1, 0, −1.

2. Count through an entire deck one card at a time and keep a running count.

For a single deck, the running count starts at zero. As

each card is played, you need to recall its value and add that to the running count. Again, this must be done completely silently and with no lip movement. If you make no mistakes, your RC will be +4 at the end of the deck. For the example above, the same sequence of cards would be counted in the following fashion.

Single Card	K-O Value	Running Count
3	+1	+1
5	+1	+2
king	−1	+1
2	+1	+2
8	0	+2
queen	−1	+1

3. Practice with pairs of cards.

When you've become comfortable keeping the count, practice by turning the cards over two at a time and determining the net count for each pair of cards. For example, a hand of jack and ace (a blackjack) has a net count equal to $(-1) + (-1) = -2$. Two tens also have a net Knock-Out count value of -2. A stiff total of 16 made up of Q,6 has a net count equal to $(-1) + (+1) = 0$.

Practice this until counting pairs is second-nature and you don't need to do the addition. Strive to recognize pairs that cancel to zero, such as 10,2, Q,4, A,5, etc. This canceling technique will save you a great deal of effort and greatly increase your speed.

4. Count through an entire deck in pairs while keeping a running count.

Turning two cards over at a time, you need to recall (not calculate) their net Knock-Out value, and add it to the running count. For our card sequence above, we would count in the following fashion.

Pair of Cards	Net K-O Value	Running Count
3,5	+2	+2
K,2	0	+2
8,Q	−1	+1

How fast do you need to be? A good rule of thumb, no matter which card-counting system you use, is to be able to count down an entire deck of cards in 25 to 30 seconds.

Many beginners find the prospect of counting an entire deck in 30 seconds a bit daunting. Don't worry. Once you master the technique of netting (and canceling) two cards at a time, you'll literally fly through the deck. In a short amount of time, counting cards will become as easy as reading. When you read words, you don't recite the sound of each letter and you don't try to sound out the word. You simply view the word and your brain immediately recognizes it. The same will happen with card counting after some practice.

Once you can count one deck, the transition to multiple decks isn't difficult. The only change is the new value for the initial running count, which is necessary to ensure that you always end up with a final RC of +4.

We recommend practicing with the number of decks that you will most often play against. For example, if you live on the East Coast and know you'll be visiting Atlantic City or Foxwoods, you'll be best served practicing for the 6- and 8-deck shoes that you'll encounter in those destinations. The same is true for patrons of Midwestern and Southern riverboat casinos. On the other hand, visitors to Nevada will have a choice of several different games, and may want to become proficient counting both single and multiple decks.

To succeed in casino-like conditions, you must be able to count the entire pack quickly *and* correctly. If you're too slow, you won't be able to keep track of all the cards in a casino environment. Counting only a fraction of the cards is self-destructive, as you aren't making use of all the information

SPEED AT THE TABLES

In actual play, you should strive to be able to count a table full of cards in a few seconds. While this may sound formidable, you'll find that it's easier done than said.

Remember first that all cards of zero value are ignored. Thus, all 8s and 9s can be disregarded. Next, combinations of cards with a total value of zero can also be ignored. If you see somebody stand with a hand of K,7, you simply ignore the net count of zero. Similarly, a hand with J,6 that hits and busts with an 8 can also be ignored.

Eventually, you'll be able to cancel cards that are in adjacent hands. For example, with three adjacent hands of a J,Q, a 4,8,8, and a 3,9,Q, you might view it as follows. Ignore the 8s and 9; the 3 and queen in the third hand cancel. What's left is two −1 cards (the jack and queen) and one +1 card (the 4). The jack cancels the 4, leaving only the queen unaccounted for. Hence, the net count for this group is simply that of the queen: −1. With a little practice at thinking like this, you'll be able to glance at a group of five to ten cards and quickly determine the net count for the group.

available to you. Far worse is counting only a fraction of the cards and consistently missing the same *type* of card.

Let's take an example where you're just a little slow and seem to miss counting a player's last card when he busts. This is a reasonable scenario, since dealers tend to snatch up the cards from a busted hand quickly. Missing (or neglecting) this card will cut into profits in two major ways. First, you won't count about one in every 15 cards dealt, which has negative consequences with regard to effective deck penetration (a factor in profitability that will be discussed later in the text).

Second, and far more damaging, your count will become an inaccurate indicator, signaling you to increase your bet at inopportune times. Why? Hands tend to bust with high cards. Always missing these cards (which are preferentially negative in their count values) will greatly inflate your running count, causing you to incorrectly conclude that you have the advantage when you don't. Not only will you suffer from inaccurate betting, you'll compound the error by playing key hands wrong.

SUMMARY

• The Knock-Out system eliminates, or greatly simplifies, most tasks associated with successful card counting. The K-O is a single-level, single-parameter, unbalanced count, which means that no true-count conversion is necessary—the count is started at the IRC, and decisions made according to the running count only.

• You must learn to keep the running count perfectly. This will require practice. In time, you will learn to recognize the K-O values instantly and update the count automatically.

• The information the running count provides allows you to make proper betting and playing decisions. The techniques for using this information are described in the chapters that follow.

Round 5

The Knock-Out System— Rookie

Eureka! I have found it.
—Archimedes

It's time to start putting what we've learned to practical use. As we've made clear throughout this book, the K-O system was designed to incorporate the best combination of strength and ease of use. It's powerful and it's easy—but it's not a "gimme." To capture the full potential of the system (and maximize your earnings), you'll have to study and practice. That said, however, we're at a point, right now, at which we can use our knowledge to actually play the game of blackjack with an advantage over the mighty house.

The K-O Rookie system, presented here, is a streamlined ultra-simple manifestation of the K-O technique. But it's also something more. In the purest sense, K-O Rookie is the essence of winning blackjack. That's because winning at blackjack, more than anything else, is about bet variation—betting a lot when you have the advantage and betting a little when you don't. The K-O Rookie system shows you how to do exactly that.

Two subsets of players will benefit from this incarnation of the K-O counting system. The first consists of novice counters who find the initiation into the casino environment somewhat overwhelming. Playing "for real," with real money and real distractions, often turns out to be quite daunting. Because of this, we've found that card counters making their debut in casinos sometimes do better starting with an extremely simple approach.

The second subset comprises a much larger group. It's made up of thousands of players who have learned (or partially learned) basic strategy, but either can't or won't learn to count cards; they've been convinced that counting is too difficult. Many of these players know intuitively that in order to win they have to raise their bets at some point during play—if they don't, the house edge will grind them down and, eventually, out. But at what point do you raise?

The only time it's truly correct to raise your bet is when you have an advantage over the house, and those times can only be identified by counting cards. Since most players don't count, they turn to other means to guide their betting. Most rely on "money-management" techniques. There's only one problem with this approach: it doesn't work. You cannot overcome the casino's advantage at blackjack with bet variation that *isn't correlated* with the count. Blackjack players using basic strategy along with such betting systems can expect to lose at a rate equal to the house advantage—no more and no less.

Knock-Out Rookie is a betting system, too. But it's a choreographed system that *is correlated* with the count.

By combining perfect basic strategy play and the ability to keep the running count (perfected by the techniques in Chapter 4) with the betting advice in this chapter, you can play blackjack with an advantage. It's time to find out how.

ANOTHER LOOK AT THE KEY COUNT

Recall the gumball analogy (Chapter 3) in which we introduced the concept of the key count. The key count is the count at which we first have the advantage. It was +1 in the gumball game, which signified that there was one extra winning gumball in the mix and favorable for us to raise our bet.

It works the same way when playing blackjack. Instead of counting gumballs, though, we count the cards according to the K-O values. We then monitor the running count as we play, betting small when the RC is below the key count, and betting big when it's at or above the key count.

It's that simple. There are only two bets, small and large, and the key count is the point that separates them. The chart below lists the two crucial numbers you need to know: the IRC and the key count. (Note: Refer to Chapter 4 for the equation to derive the standard IRCs for games not listed, and Appendix 7 for data on 4-deck games.)

KNOCK-OUT SYSTEM
STANDARD IRCS AND KEY COUNTS

Conditions	IRC	Key Count
1 deck	0	+2
2 decks	−4	+1
6 decks	−20	−4
8 decks	−28	−6

What constitutes big and small in your betting scheme? It's a matter of personal preference, as well as a function of your gambling bankroll, your aversion to risk, and so forth. You might choose the table minimum, say $5, for your small bet. A $5 wager thus represents a 1-unit bet. Your big bet will then be the multiple of $5 that you choose. For example, if your big bet is $25 (5 × $5), you'll be employing a 1-5 "spread."

BENCHMARKS

In order to gauge the effectiveness of the strategies presented in this book, it's necessary to create benchmarks for comparison. The performance results presented henceforth assume perfect play (no betting or playing-strategy errors) and the conditions listed here.

1 deck: H17, DOA, noDAS, 65% penetration
2 decks: S17, DOA, no DAS, 75% penetration
6 decks: S17, DOA, no DAS, 75% penetration
8 decks: S17, DOA, no DAS, 75% penetration

A COMPLETE SYSTEM

In essence, we now have the makings of a complete blackjack system. For playing we use the basic strategy as presented in Chapter 2. For betting, we use the K-O card-counting method and bet one of two values: We wager 1 unit below the key count, and X units at or above the key count, where X is an amount greater than 1 unit. Everything else about how we play the game remains the same. We've dubbed this system "K-O Rookie" because it's the most basic application of the concept of varying your bet according to the count. Still, with a big enough "jump" in the bet, it's enough to beat the game.

How well do we fare with the K-O Rookie system? The table below portrays the theoretical results. The table shows a spread of 1 unit to X units, with X being either 2, 5, or 10. For example, in a single-deck game (with our benchmark rules) where you spread from 1 unit below the key count to 5 units at or above the key count, your expectation is .88% of your average initial bet.

EXPECTATION (IN %) FOR K-O ROOKIE

Decks	1-2	1-5	1-10
1	.20	.88	1.24
2	.07	.69	1.05
6	−.15	.26	.54
8	−.22	.16	.43

These results are quite impressive. An expectation of .88% means that, in the long run, you will win at a rate equal to .88% of the total initial amount of money wagered.

As you can see, greater spreads correspond to greater profits. Unfortunately, you may not be able to get away with highly profitable bet spreads for long. Moving wagers directly from 1 unit to 5 units in hand-held games and 1 to 10 in shoes is about the outside limit for bet variation unless you have a very good "act." And even at these levels, casinos may soon identify you as a winning player and take action to limit your effectiveness. You may even be barred from playing altogether (see Chapter 8 for more about the casino vs. player cat-and-mouse game).

Even at less-profitable spreads, however, K-O Rookie will get you close to breakeven or better. It's highly unlikely that anyone will stop you from going 1-2 in hand-held or 1-5 in shoe games. Even with these modest bet variations, you're no longer the underdog. You can play blackjack with an expectation of making money.

Remember, there are no strategy plays to learn; this betting method and basic strategy represent the complete Rookie version of the Knock-Out system. Casual players may not want to go any further.

FLUCTUATION PROVISO

As counters, we have the advantage when betting and playing properly. However, this does not mean that we will win each and every time we play.

Consider craps, which (for the pass line wager) has a player expectation of -1.4%. Despite this disadvantage, players sometimes win at craps in the short run. Indeed, if players never won while gambling, casinos would cease to exist. The point, however, is that in the long run, a crap player must lose.

In blackjack, the situation is reversed. While we know that we must win in the long run, in the short run we'll have fluctuations and sustain losing sessions. We must be careful, therefore, not to "overbet," lest we lose our bankroll during these negative swings. We want to be sure that we remain in the game for the long run.

To do this, you must always bet within your means. Though many players will decide how to bet based on "what they think they can get away with," severe caveats are in order for this approach. Unless your bankroll is sufficiently large to warrant this high frequency of maximum wagers, you will almost certainly go broke eventually by implementing an arbitrarily large jump spread. It's true that the bigger the jump spread you employ, the higher your expectation will be. But, an arbitrary jump spread with no regard for the size of your bankroll should be attempted only if you honestly don't mind losing the entire stake.

A good rule of thumb is to limit your maximum bet to no more than 1% of your total blackjack bankroll. For example, if your bankroll is $10,000, then your max bet might be $100. Keeping your maximum bet below 1% of your bankroll should reduce your risk of ruin to an acceptable level. We can't emphasize enough the danger of betting too much, even when you have the advantage (see Chapter 7 for a more detailed discussion of this crucial concept).

CUSTOMIZING

If you have an aversion to working with negative numbers, we highly recommend that you customize the count. Customizing means tailoring the IRC and key count values, and it can be done so that you never have to count with negative numbers. It's an easy process that's explained in Appendix 8, along with a specific example of a count customized for the K-O Rookie.

THE K-O ROOKIE IN GAME CONDITIONS

Let's assume we're playing head-up in a 2-deck game. For a double deck, the IRC is −4 and the key count is +1. We'll employ the K-O Rookie system with a unit of $5 and a spread of 1 to 3 units.

The dealer shuffles and we're ready to go. At the start, the running count is the same as the initial running count of −4, so we bet just $5. The cards come out and we're dealt 5,6 while the dealer has a 4 up. Following basic strategy, we double down, and receive a 9 for a total of 20. The dealer turns over the downcard, a queen, and draws an 8 to bust. We win $10 ($5 for the original wager and $5 for the double). The RC is now –2.

Because the RC of –2 is still below the key count, we again bet $5. This time we're dealt 8,8 and the dealer has a 6 up. As prescribed by the basic strategy, we split our 8s. On the first hand we're dealt a jack and stand. On the second we receive a 5 and stand. The dealer turns over a 6 (for a total of 12) and hits the hand with a 7 for a total of 19. We lose $10 ($5 on each of our split hands) this round. Now the RC is +1, which is equal to the key count. We have the advantage! We go ahead and bet $15. May the cards be with us.

SUMMARY

• K-O Rookie is the simplest incarnation of the Knock-Out system. For betting, we count according to the K-O card values and jump our bet at or above the key count. For strategy, we play according to the basic strategy.

• There are several easy ways to enhance the K-O Rookie system. This takes us to the K-O Preferred system, presented in the next chapter.

Round 6

The Knock-Out System— Preferred Strategy

(Casinos) make their living encouraging people to believe in systems, in luck, cultivating the notion that some people are better gamblers than others, that there is a savvy, macho personality that can force dame fortune to obey his will.
—Peter Griffin, THE THEORY OF BLACKJACK

Reaching the point where we have the advantage represents the realization of a big part of our goal. However, we can do considerably better with just a little additional effort. The remainder of this book is for players who want to go farther, possibly to the expert level, and maybe even to professional status.

In this chapter, we'll incorporate a playing strategy that tells us when it's proper to play our hand in a manner other than by basic strategy, and in Chapter 7, we'll refine our betting technique relative to what the Knock-Out count is able to tell us. The eventual combining of these improved playing and betting strategies will create what we call the "Knock-Out Preferred" system. For convenience, however, we'll refer to any version of the K-O strategy with enhancements beyond K-O Rookie as K-O Preferred.

The Knock-Out Preferred system presented here conforms to our objective of providing the greatest gain in power for the least increase in difficulty. And to allow maximum flexibility, we present the Preferred version in a form that lets you choose exactly which strategic plays you want to memorize, which means you can decide which level of complexity to adopt.

The Preferred Strategy version of the K-O system employs a "reduced and rounded" strategy matrix, which retains nearly 95% of the possible theoretical gain (over basic strategy alone) from using the "Full" Knock-Out system. (The Full K-O system is discussed in Appendix 4). The matrix is "reduced" in the sense that we use only the 18 strategic plays that provide the most gain for the player. Balanced-count aficionados may note the similarity in concept with Don Schlesinger's "Illustrious 18."[31] The matrix is "rounded" in that entries are not described by a range of integer values. Indeed, regardless of the number of decks being dealt, there are only three possible matrix values to remember in the K-O Preferred system.

One quick reminder. Recall that one of the K-O count's important references is called the pivot point. We discussed the pivot briefly in Chapter 3, and will discuss it in more detail (in connection with improved betting strategies) in Chapter 7. For now, though, you need only be aware that it exists, since it will be referenced in the strategy matrix. This should not present much difficulty, since the pivot point is *always* +4.[32]

The K-O Preferred strategy matrix is presented on page 85. But first, we'll learn a single strategy play that you can add to your arsenal immediately. It's the proper play of insurance.

---

[31] See Donald Schlesinger's "Attacking the Shoe," in *Blackjack Forum*, September 1986.

[32] Most of the strategy plays are triggered by reaching the pivot point, since this is the point at which we have reliable information about the magnitude of our advantage, and the content of the remaining deck.

K-O PREFERRED INSURANCE

The most important strategic play in the K-O system is insurance. You probably recall that the proper basic strategy play is to *never* take insurance. So what's the deal?

Well, we're counting cards now, which provides us with additional information about the remaining deck content. Just as the key count provides useful information about when to bet more, so too can we extract information relative to when it's proper to take insurance.

It turns out that the insurance wager becomes profitable to us when the standard K-O running count is greater than or equal to +3. Conveniently, this is true regardless of the number of decks in use. Whether we are playing at a single-deck or an 8-deck game, if we have the opportunity to take insurance and the present standard RC is +3 or more, we make the insurance wager.

For example, let's say you're in a single-deck game. It's the first hand after the shuffle. The player next to you is dealt 6,5. You hold 2,7, and the dealer shows an ace as the upcard. Should you take insurance? The IRC for this game is 0, but with the five cards visible the running count is now exactly +3. In this case then, the answer is yes, you should take insurance. Always remember to count every card you can see, including the dealer's upcard, before making this play (or any strategic playing decision).

How much does the inclusion of the insurance play gain you? The table on page 84 shows the improvement in expectation for adding this insurance play to the strategy used for the K-O Rookie system. By comparing the table with the table on page 77, you can readily see how much is gained for the different betting scenarios. Making correct insurance decisions is more valuable with bigger bet spreads and in games with fewer decks. It's worth .2% in a single-deck game with a 1-10 bet spread, but essentially nothing in the 8-deck game.

EXPECTATION (IN %) FOR K-O PREFERRED
VERSION: INSURANCE ONLY

Decks	1-2	1-5	1-10
1	.33	1.06	1.44
2	.15	.80	1.18
6	−.15	.27	.55
8	−.22	.16	.43

THE K-O PREFERRED: TOTAL STRATEGY

The remainder of the K-O Preferred strategy matrix is presented on page 85. How do you use this sparse-looking table?

In reality, the strategy is still very similar to the basic strategy. As mentioned, of the 270 basic strategy plays, a mere 18 exceptions (those with entries denoted *A*, *B*, and *C*, plus insurance) exist in the Preferred K-O system. This can be contrasted with the Hi-Opt I or High-Low systems, which in full form contain 50 to 150 matrix decisions to memorize, each of which can take on one of 13 or more integers. Ouch!

The similarity allows us to present only the portion of the Preferred strategy matrix that's different from the basic strategy. All splitting decisions (not shown) and soft-hand decisions (not shown) are made *exactly* in accordance with the basic strategy. For the portion of the matrix that is shown, all entries with a blank box also revert back to the basic strategy play. For example, we stand with a hard 14 vs. a dealer 2, just as basic strategy prescribes. We hit with a hard 16 vs. a dealer 8, again just as before.

The remaining 17 entries, denoted with *A*, *B*, and *C*, represent the complete Preferred Strategy matrix. For these plays, we follow the legend. For example, if holding a hard 16 vs. a dealer ten, we stand if the running count is greater than or

KNOCK-OUT
PREFERRED STRATEGY MATRIX

Dealer's Upcard

Player's Hand	2	3	4	5	6	7	8	9	10	A
Hard 17 ↑										
Hard 16								A	B	
Hard 15									A	
Hard 14										
Hard 13	C	C								
Hard 12	A	A	C	C	C					
11										A
10									A	A
9	A					A				
8 ↓				A	A					

	Category *A*	Category *B*	Category *C*
1 deck	*+4*	*+2*	*0*
2 deck	*+4*	*+1*	*–4*
6 deck	*+4*	*–4*	*Omit*
8 deck	*+4*	*–6*	*Omit*

Play all soft hands, pairs, and blanks according to the basic strategy. Take insurance at running count ≥ 3.

Hard 12↑ *Value* = stand if RC ≥ *Value*; otherwise hit.

  11↓ *Value* = double down if RC ≥ *Value*; otherwise hit.

tion.[33] Following the table is Figure 5, which charts the cumulative gain from each of the strategic plays for our model. We have enumerated the plays in accordance with the table.

As you can see, the single most useful strategy play to memorize is the proper play of insurance—which is why only this play was categorized separately. The next most important play is 16 vs. a dealer ten, etc. In general, the most important plays are from category *A* for the reasons discussed above.

The set of 18 plays makes up the Preferred Strategy version of the Knock-Out system, but you need not memorize all 18. If you choose to memorize, say, only four matrix plays, then the following table and figure indicate the most valuable quartet that should be memorized: insurance, 16 vs. ten, 15 vs. ten, and then 12 vs. 3.

In this way, the system can be personalized for your needs and/or inclinations. Customize the system to suit yourself. Remember though, that the more strategy plays you memorize, the higher your expectation will be.

Even if you use all 18 strategy plays, it's still less memorization than is required in other popular systems, or even the many numerical values in the "Illustrious 18" of a balanced system.

APPLYING THE PREFERRED STRATEGY TABLE

Consider the entry for hard 16 vs. a dealer 9. The Preferred strategy matrix entry is *A*, meaning we stand if the running count is greater than or equal to this value, and hit otherwise. Regardless of the number of decks in play, the

---

[33] This representative ordering assumes 2 decks and a moderate ramp and bet spread. The ordering will vary as these conditions change.

Strategy Number	Strategy Play	Strategy Number	Strategy Play
1	Insurance	10	10 vs. ace
2	16 vs. ten	11	9 vs. 7
3	15 vs. ten	12	8 vs. 6
4	12 vs. 3	13	16 vs. 9
5	10 vs. ten	14	13 vs. 2
6	11 vs. ace	15	8 vs. 5
7	12 vs. 2	16	12 vs. 5
8	12 vs. 4	17	12 vs. 6
9	9 vs. 2	18	13 vs. 3

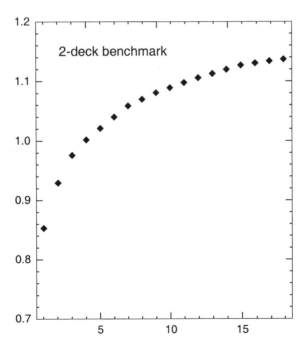

Figure 5: *Cumulative value of each of the 18 Preferred strategic plays for the Knock-Out system as applied in a 2-deck game, using the benchmark 1-5 spread with a ramp of 3 (the spread and ramp used for this model are defined in Chapter 7).*

value of A is always +4. This means that if we're holding a hard 16 and the dealer has a 9 up, we stand if the RC is +4 or more; otherwise we hit.

Is this logical? Recall that basic strategy for this play is to hit. We'd expect to deviate from the basic strategy and stand if there were a large fraction of high cards left in the deck. Our +4 pivot indicates that a large number of high cards remain. Since our chance of busting is large, it makes sense in this case to stand.

A study of the other strategic plays will convince you that these, too, are made only at opportune (and logical) times. In particular, most of the double downs are made when the count is high and there's a correspondingly high chance of drawing a ten to the doubled hand.

K-O PREFERRED STRATEGY EXPECTATION

Using the K-O Preferred with the complete strategy matrix and a jump spread at the key count for betting, the performance is as follows. Notice the improvement over the Rookie system in all games.

EXPECTATION (IN %) FOR K-O PREFERRED
VERSION: STRATEGY MATRIX

Decks	1-2	1-5	1-10
1	.61	1.40	1.80
2	.33	1.04	1.43
6	−.09	.36	.66
8	−.18	.22	.52

LATE SURRENDER

Late surrender (when available) is another option that can be used to good advantage. As a reminder, late surrender is an option by which you may forfeit half of your wager before playing out a bad hand, so long as the dealer does not have a natural. Surrender, when proper, takes precedence over all other possible options.

KNOCK-OUT PREFERRED LATE SURRENDER MATRIX

Dealer's Upcard

Player's Hand	8	9	10	A
HARD 16	*A*	Su	Su	Su
HARD 15		*A*	Su	*A*
HARD 14			*A*	*A*

Surrender if RC ≥ *Value*; otherwise hit.
Surrender 8,8 vs. a dealer ten at *B*.

ADDITIONAL TIPS

Regardless of how much of the K-O Preferred system you choose to incorporate into your play, the strategy tables should not be viewed as a completely new aspect of the system. Certainly this is true if you use only the insurance play made at a sufficiently high running count of +3 or more. But even in the Preferred version, the strategy matrices should be thought of merely as an extension of the basic strategy. Most of the decisions you'll make, even when counting, will be exactly the same as the basic strategy.

For whatever situation you find yourself in, you must be able to instantly recall the correct strategy entry. Two situations in particular illustrate why.

First, when playing "head-up" with the dealer (you are the only player at the table), the pace of the game can be quite rapid. This is a situation that you should strive for, as it results in more hands per hour and, hence, more profits. However, you must be able to keep up with the dealer to take advantage of it. It's true that you can play slowly, and the dealer will eventually get into your rhythm and decelerate the pace, but this defeats the primary purpose of playing head-up.

A second time that instant recall is needed is when you're drawing to a multiple-card hand. Dealers expect you to complete your decision-making quickly once a hand is in progress, so you have to calculate your total and determine the correct play within a split second.

Remember also that you can customize K-O with a chosen IRC, key count, or pivot point in mind (see Appendix 8).

One last piece of advice: Count every card you see up until your decision. The more cards that are included in your RC, the more accurate your play will be. A quick example. Let's assume that the RC at the start of a hand is +5. You make a large wager and are dealt J,Q. But the dealer has an ace up. Should you take insurance? Well, you might think insurance is warranted since the RC at the beginning of the hand was +5, but making the insurance bet would be incorrect. The updated RC, which includes your jack, queen, and the dealer's ace, is +2; hence you should decline the insurance bet.

SUMMARY

• This chapter addresses opportunities to enhance the K-O system's performance with an improved playing strategy. The Preferred Strategy incarnation of K-O employs a "reduced and rounded" matrix. The Preferred Strategy system provides an outstanding mix of simplicity and power, and can further be custom-tailored to suit an individual's desires.

• A single strategy enhancement, the proper play of insurance, can be added to improve results immediately. We take insurance whenever the running count is at or above +3, regardless of the number of decks in use.

Round 7

The Knock-Out System—
Preferred Betting

Do not follow where the path may lead.
Go instead where there is no path and
leave a trail.
　　　　　　　　　　　　　　—Unknown

In Chapter 5, we learned to use the K-O count values to size our bets from "small to big." The discussion in this chapter concentrates on enhancing our results by improving (fine-tuning) our betting tactics.

For many, this will be the most difficult chapter to follow. Still, we encourage you to read it through; for while the explanations of these "proportional betting" techniques may be daunting, the applications are not.

Before examining these betting methods, we will touch, once more, on the pivot point and the key count.

THE PIVOT POINT REVISITED

We talked about the pivot point in Chapter 3, and briefly again in Chapter 6. Recall that when the running count is at the pivot point, we have good information regarding our actual expectation. Stated another way, unbalanced systems such as K-O are constructed so the pivot point coincides with a known player advantage. As such, it serves as a reliable reference to correlate our betting with our advantage.

Assume we're playing a 2-deck game, and that after one half of a deck (26 cards) is dealt out the running count is +4 (instead of the expected average value of –2; see figure 4, pg. 67). What would an equivalent true count be? Well, the excess count is +4 – (–2) = +6. That is, we are +6 above where we expect to be, on average.

The number of decks remaining is 1.5. Therefore, the true count is +6/1.5 = +4. So you see, at the pivot point of +4, the K-O running count is always exactly equal to a K-O true count of +4. This relationship holds true regardless of the number of decks in play or the number of cards already dealt out, so long as the Knock-Out IRC is calculated as prescribed.[34]

What does this gain for us as practitioners of the K-O system? Well, it means that when we have a running count of +4, we have a very good idea of where we stand because we know, to a high degree of certainty, the expectation at a true count of +4. Remember that the true count is an accurate measure of the prevailing expectation. So when the K-O running count is at the pivot point of +4, we have good information about our expectation, regardless of how many cards remain to be played.[35]

---

[34] This relationship is also approximately true when comparing K-O to a balanced count. Orthodox balanced-system students may correctly object that there is no equivalent balanced system to an unbalanced system. However, we argue here only that a similar balanced system (e.g., 2 through 7 = +1; 8 through 9 = 0; 10 through ace = –1.2) will yield the desired relation.

[35] See Peter Griffin's *The Theory of Blackjack* for a proof of the conjecture that the expectation, as derived from an unbalanced count at the pivot point, is independent of the number of cards left to be played. Only at the pivot point is this strictly true.

Then, based on a change in expectation of about +0.55% per unit of true count (roughly the High-Low equivalent), we find that whenever our Knock-Out RC is at the pivot point of +4, our expectation is approximately $4 \times 0.55\% = 2.2\%$ above the starting basic strategy expectation. For a 6-deck game with standard rules, for example, our expectation at the pivot is nearly +1.8%, after accounting for the basic strategy expectation of about –0.4%.

THE KEY COUNT REVISITED

As we know, the key count is the running count at which we first have the advantage. Fortunately, in the K-O system the key count is a function only of the number of decks in play and little else. This is true for all sets of rules you're likely to encounter.

We can determine the key counts empirically by simulating the K-O system and looking at the expectation as a function of the running count. Consider Figure 6 (pg. 98) derived via simulation.

Clearly, if your goal is to make money, the best strategy would be to avoid all hands with a negative expectation. Just skip them altogether and play only when the playin's good! If adopting this strategy in, let's say, a 2-deck game, then we would count down the deck as it's being played. Whenever the running count got to +1 (the key count) or more, we would jump in and play. If the running count was 0 or less, we would sit out the next round. In this way, we would be playing only in positive-expectation situations.

We can also estimate the relative value of a one-point change in the running count once we have the advantage. In such favorable situations, we find the results listed on page 99.

Some readers may be surprised by the magnitude of the change in a single-deck game. Remember that the K-O has

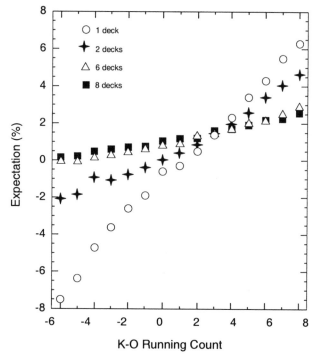

Figure 6: *The expectation as a function of K-O running count. Recall that the key count is the count at or above which the expectation is positive. Thus, for a single-deck game, the key count is +2, and so forth. Note that the expectation changes in roughly a linear fashion with the running count, and also that there is a tight correlation in expectation at and near the pivot point of +4.*

no true-count conversion. Thus, the change in expectation represents an average over the prevailing conditions. A typical card removed from a single deck will change the expectation by about 0.45%. A card removed from only half a deck will change the expectation by about twice as much, and so on. When these effects are averaged over a single-deck game with 65% penetration, we wind up with an average effect of 0.9%. The same type of reasoning can be used to understand the rest of the table.

APPROXIMATE EFFECT OF ONE-POINT CHANGE
IN FAVORABLE RUNNING COUNT

Game	Change in Expectation (%)
1 deck	0.90
2 decks	0.60
6 decks	0.20
8 decks	0.15

BETTING

Unfortunately, most casinos don't allow you to exit and re-enter a game at will. Sitting at a table and playing a few hands, sitting out a few, then jumping in and playing again is a sure-fire way to draw attention to yourself.

A less obvious way to play is to back-count, which means standing behind a table and counting cards until a favorable situation arises, then jumping in with a big wager. This approach was first suggested by Thorp and is now sometimes referred to as "wonging." Back-counting makes you less obvious in your avoidance of the negative hands at the beginning of the pack while you wait to play only the positive hands thereafter. As soon as the deck sours, you leave to find another table.

But casinos have started to thwart back-counters as well. In fact, many now do not allow mid-shoe entry. Only players who have participated since the very first hand out of the shoe are allowed to continue to play until the dealer reshuffles. Another way to play is front-counting, where you leave the game when the count gets sufficiently negative. In Chapter 8, we will discuss this further and present a K-O exit strategy for shoe games.

The point is, casino conditions today ensure that having to play during negative counts is almost unavoidable. This is especially true for casual players. If we have to play every hand, then we need to have a plan.

KELLY BETTING

The plan, it turns out, is the same as it has been: Bet big when we have the advantage and bet small when we don't. Only now we would like to correlate the size of our big bets more closely with the size of our advantage.

The question is how to quantify the betting scheme. Kelly[36] has determined that the optimal method of betting, so as to minimize the chance of ruin and "maximize profits,"[37] is to wager an amount that's proportional to your current capital. The constant of proportionality, or "ramp" factor, turns out to be equal to (slightly less than) the percentage of your advantage.[38]

Kelly wagering requires that you constantly re-evaluate your present bankroll in order to properly calibrate the next wager. The "Kelly Criterion" method of wagering therefore presses up the bet sizes of an increasing bankroll at opportune times *when the player has the advantage* (not just because the bankroll is increasing), and also limits the potential of "gambler's ruin" by decreasing wagers when the bankroll is dwindling.

---

[36] J. L. Kelly, "A New Interpretation of Information Rate," *IRE Transactions on Information Theory—Bell System Technical Journal*, 1956, Vol. 35, 917.

[37] Kelly seeks to maximize a so-called utility function equal to the logarithm of the expected bankroll.

[38] Optimally, we'd like to bet 0 when we are at a disadvantage, but we'll assume here that we must make some minimum bet.

MODIFIED PROPORTIONAL BETTING

Optimal Kelly wagering requires precise bet sizing (which can result in wagers in fractions of a chip). Though powerful in theory, in practice, perfect Kelly betting is not realistic. A somewhat more practical approach to betting is a method referred to as "modified proportional betting." The wagering is still quasi-Kelly, but there are important differences. First, it's assumed that any win or loss for a playing session is small compared to the entire bankroll. This way, the bankroll need not be re-evaluated prior to every wager. Before a session begins, the bankroll can be evaluated once and bet sizes predetermined for the entire session.

Furthermore, bets are capped at a maximum level we'll call the "ceiling." Ideally, we'd like to bet proportionally (to our advantage) no matter how high the expectation rises. In practice, however, we cannot get away with spreading from, say, 1 to 100 units, even though the count may merit it. In the casino, we must have a ceiling at some point, if only because of the table limit. The range of the floor to ceiling levels is commonly called the "bet spread."

It's always somewhat problematic to develop a benchmark for determining the performance of a card-counting system (for purposes of comparing with other systems). For this book, we've chosen to use a modified proportional betting comparison, which places the respective systems on a similar scale in terms of risk of ruin.

Assuming a modified proportional betting scheme is the appropriate vehicle of comparison, two important variables must be determined. First, what is the bet spread? Second, how quickly does the wagering traverse the bet spread?

We've already touched on some of the interesting ramifications of choosing and attempting to implement a bet spread. Ideally, we'd like to use an infinite spread. But again, in practice this isn't possible. We believe a reasonable bet spread for which counters should strive is 1 to 5 in a single- or double-deck game, and 1 to 10 in 6- and 8-deck games.

Traversing the bet spread is a concept that also merits further attention. The issue here is how fast we change our wagering from the minimum (at a disadvantage) to the maximum (with the advantage). With a finite bankroll, we'll move up and down with our bets in direct proportion to our prevailing expectation (a la Kelly). The slope of the ramp is proportional to our starting bankroll, with a greater bankroll implying a steeper ramp (we'll make more maximum bets).

RULE AND BETTING BENCHMARKS

Following are the rules and benchmarks we use to derive the performance results in this chapter.

Single deck: H17, DOA, noDAS, 65% penetration;
Spread 1 to 5 with ramp of 3

Double deck: S17, DOA, noDAS, 75% penetration;
Spread 1 to 5 with ramp of 3

Six deck: S17, DOA, DAS, 75% penetration;
Spread 1 to 10 with ramp of 6

Eight deck: S17, DOA, DAS, 75% penetration;
Spread 1 to 10 with ramp of 6

We have used what we believe to be ramping values which have a reasonable chance of being implemented, or at least approximately so, in actual casino play. Consider the 2-deck game with a spread of 1 to 5. The minimum wager is 1 unit, while the maximum is 5 units. In between, our simulation has the wagers rise linearly in proportion to the expectation based on the running count. The ramp factor we have chosen is 3.[39]

In a nutshell, this means that we try to theoretically bet 3 times the prevailing expectation as estimated from the present K-O running count. For example, when the expectation is 1.0%, we'd like to bet 3 units. When the expectation rises above +1.67%, where we want to bet more than 5 units, we stop at 5 since that is our ceiling. When the expectation falls below +0.33% where we want to bet less than 1 unit, we make the 1-unit bet since this is our floor. With this betting benchmark in the 2-deck game, we make the minimum wager roughly two-thirds of the time, and the maximum wager about 15% of the time. The average wager in this 2-deck benchmark is roughly 2 units.

In real-world conditions, you're not allowed to bet fractions of a dollar. Therefore, a specific "integer" spread has been used to determine bet sizing at different counts for the analysis of the complete K-O Preferred count system. The betting schemes used are portrayed below; each follows closely the theoretical benchmark outlined above.

Single Deck—Betting Progression I

RC	0⇓	+1	+2	+3	+4⇑
Bet	1	1	2	4	5

---

[39] We note that the final results are somewhat sensitive to the ramping factor and bet spread. However, especially in comparisons among systems as presented in Appendix 3, these variables have little effect on relative performance.

2 Decks—Betting Progression II

RC	0⇓	+1	+2	+3	+4⇑
Bet	1	2	3	4	5

6 Decks—Betting Progression VI

RC	−5⇓	−4	−3	−2	−1	0	+1	+2
Bet	1	2	2	3	4	5	6	8

	+3	+4⇑
	9	10

8 Decks—Betting Progression VIII

RC	−7⇓	−6	−5	−4	−3	−2	−1	0
Bet	1	2	2	2	3	4	5	6

	+1	+2	+3	+4⇑
	7	8	9	10

THE K-O PREFERRED EXPECTATION

We can now get a handle on the expectation for applying the complete Knock-Out Preferred system. It's important to realize that this is not an apples-to-apples comparison with K-O Rookie, K-O Preferred Strategy, etc., whose derivations of expectation were based on the two-bet (small and big) jump spread. That's because the complete K-O Preferred derivation is based on a proportional betting approach with intermediate betting values that conform to our benchmark and betting scheme.

A comparison of these returns with those in the table on page 90 reveals that there's a slight gain in expectation (except in the 8-deck game) for implementing a proportional wagering

EXPECTATION (IN %) FOR
COMPLETE K-O PREFERRED

Decks	1-5	1-10
1	1.53	
2	1.11	
6		.73
8		.52

scheme. The primary benefit from this technique, however, is related to risk, as the proportional approach conforms more closely to Kelly wagering. The graduated bet increases will also provide a little more cover, as opposed to the drastic variation of the jump spread.

Note also that this integer spread performs almost identically to the so-called "full-fractional" betting scheme, which is essentially a best "theoretical" result. The returns for the full-fractional approach for 1, 2, 6, and 8 decks are 1.53%, 1.14%, .73%, and .54%, respectively. (These results are based on Monte Carlo simulations and have an associated error of roughly .01%. Full-fractional betting is employed for the comparisons in Appendix 3.)

PRACTICAL BETTING SCHEMES

Any betting scheme patterned after our benchmark will produce an expectation similar to that portrayed here. You can, therefore, create a model that's easy for you to implement. To formulate a practical betting scheme that's suitable for real-world applications, we are bound by two overriding concerns. First, we need to be aware of the key count. As we learned in Chapter 5, it makes sense to begin increasing our wagers once the running count is equal to the key count. Second, we'd like the ceiling (maximum bet) to be made at or near the pivot point, where we know our advantage is nearly +2%. In between the key count and the pivot point, wagers can be made in any manner—as long as they generally increase as the running count increases.

Your betting scheme does not have to be overly rigid, however. In the 2-deck schedule, you could go from 2 units at the key count to 5 units at the pivot point and float randomly from 3 to 4 units in-between, and give up very little. The plethora of betting schemes is limited only by your imagination, and by what you think you can get away with. That is, as long as you have the proper size bankroll to support it. It's always most important to pick a betting spread and ramp that you and your bankroll can live with.

RISK OF RUIN

There's a common misconception that card counters always win. Over short periods, such as days, weeks, even a couple of months, it's not a given that a skilled card counter will be ahead. In fact, the card counter could be well behind.

What's true is that given sufficient time and a sufficient bankroll, the card counter *will* eventually turn his fortune around and show a profit. This becomes close to a mathematical certainty the longer a counter plays. Let's get back to short run, however, which is quite another story.

Let's say we're playing our 2-deck game and spreading 1 to 5 units (regardless of our current bankroll). We're using the top 16 plays of the K-O Preferred matrix for strategic decisions, and we will play until either doubling our bankroll or going broke. Not surprisingly, the larger our bankroll, the more certain it is that we will succeed.

Consider Figure 7, which demonstrates this effect. No-

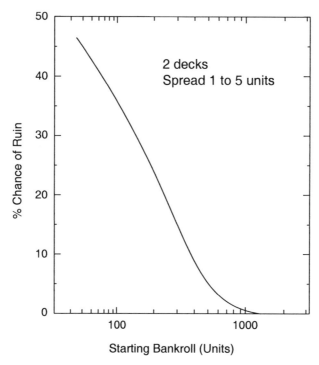

Figure 7: *The risk of ruin as a function of initial bankroll. The curve was generated assuming a 2-deck benchmark game with a spread of 1 to 5 units and a ramp of 3, using the top 16 plays of the K-O Preferred system, with the aim of doubling the bankroll before going broke.*

tice that the risk of ruin drops substantially as the initial bankroll increases. For example, with a starting bankroll of 25 units (at the spread of 1 to 5 units), the chance of success is about 53%. That is, if you sit down at a 2-deck table, buy in for $25, and spread $1 to $5 (or, alternatively, buy in for $500 while spreading $20 to $100, etc.) while using the Preferred system, you'll have about a 47% chance of going broke before doubling your money. On the other hand, if you start with 100 units, your chance of failure falls to 36%. Indeed, it nose-dives to a mere 0.5% if you start with 1,000 units, and nearly 0% for a bankroll greater than 1,500 units.

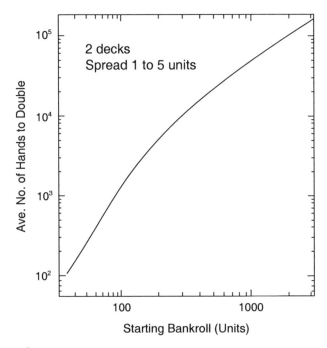

Figure 8: *This companion to Figure 7 shows the average number of hands needed to double a bankroll as a function of initial bankroll. The curve assumes a 2-deck benchmark game spreading 1 to 5 units with a ramp of 3, using the top 16 plays of the K-O Preferred system.*

Figure 8 depicts the average number of hands needed to double the bankroll.

For example, the average number of hands needed to successfully double the bankroll (on the occasions when successful) is only 100 with a starting bankroll of 25 units. The average total rises quite rapidly, approaching 1,400 hands for an initial bankroll of 100 units, and more than 21,000 hands for a bankroll of 500 units.

Let's go back to our example of an initial bankroll of 1,000 units. We know that we have a 99.5% chance of doubling the bank, which seems conservative enough. But how long will it take? The chart tells us that it will take an average of roughly 45,000 hands. Playing at the brisk rate of 100 hands per hour, that's 450 hours of play.

Do you have the time and patience for this? If not, you'll have to make some adjustments in your goals. There's a well-correlated trade-off between risk tolerance and patience. That is, quicker success comes at the expense of more risk. Where's the happy medium? Well, that's up to you. Let's look at an example.

We'll assume we have a bankroll of $5,000, and we'll use a $5 to $25 spread (1 to 5 units). This is a 1,000-unit bankroll. We know that our chance of doubling the bankroll is about 99.5%, but it will take about 450 hours.

What if we choose a $10 to $50 spread? Now our $5,000 represents a starting bankroll of 500 units. Our chance of doubling the bankroll falls to 95%, but the average doubling time also falls to only 210 hours.

Or if we're even less patient, we may choose a $25 to $125 spread, which means that our starting bankroll equals 200 units. Now our chance of doubling is only 75%, but the average doubling time falls to only 45 hours.

The trade-off between risk and time involved is obvious. You can use Figures 7 and 8 to gauge the trade. The larger your initial starting bankroll relative to your bet spread, the more assured you will be of continually winning. However, the more risk averse you are, the longer it will take to reach your objective.

FAB FIVES CUSTOMIZED COUNT

Of course we can again customize our count. Here's an example of a count customization. We call it the "Fab Fives" strategy. Fab Fives is a 6-deck customized K-O strategy with a modified IRC. But it adds something new: a rounded Preferred matrix. For the Fab Fives, we use an IRC of –3, making the pivot point +21.

For strategy decisions, we substitute +20 for *A* and +15 for *B* in our strategy matrix. We take insurance at +20. You may have noticed that we should be substituting +21 for *A* and +13 for *B*. However, we have taken the liberty of further adjusting the Preferred matrix entries for ease of memorization. Based on the study of Appendix 5, we know this will have only a tiny effect on the overall expectation. As designated by the Preferred 6-deck matrix, we ignore the *C* value and refer to the basic strategy.

Staying with the fives theme, we ramp up our bet (when we have the advantage) starting at +15, and we make our max bet at +20, a bit earlier than in the benchmark.

The advantage with this counting scheme is that *all* matrix plays and critical betting counts are now divisible by 5. Despite the rounding, our simulation shows that the power of the Fab Fives variation is nearly the same as the standard Preferred 6-deck approach (see Appendix 8).

SUMMARY

• Betting proficiency is the most important element of playing winning blackjack. While gross bet variation based on the key count can produce a player advantage, a more finely tuned betting scheme based on the pivot point will enhance results.

• Proportional (Kelly) wagering or modified proportional wagering produce the best results, both in increased expectation and in limiting risk of ruin. There is a trade-off between the rate at which you can expect to win and your tolerance of risk. You can tailor your betting strategy to match your goals and your bankroll.

• A look back at the expectation for the different incarnations of the K-O system provides a graphic look at the gain for adding each enhancement.

EXPECTATION (IN %) FOR ALL K-O INCARNATIONS				
Decks	R	R+I	R+I+S	P
1 (1-5 spread)	.88	1.06	1.40	1.53
2 (1-5)	.69	.80	1.04	1.11
6 (1-10)	.54	.55	.66	.73
8 (1-10	.43	.43	.52	.52

R = Rookie, I = Insurance, S = Strategy, P = Preferred

Round 8

Enhancing Profits

Play long and prosper.
—Apologies to Mr. Spock

Almost all casino games have a positive expectation for the house. Hence, over time the house will win its share of total wagers and an amount arbitrarily close to what's expected given its advantage.

The money that casinos win is what pays for their spectacular entrances and lavish decor, not to mention the payroll, and of course the profits for its shareholders and investors. So important are the game revenues, many casinos still use other departments (food, rooms, etc.) as loss leaders to bring gamblers through the doors.

Given this reliance on gambling revenue, it's easy to see why casinos don't like to lose, and even easier to understand why they don't like card counting and go to great lengths to discourage it. In this chapter, we'll investigate additional methods to improve our edge, and discuss how we can exercise our advantage in the face of casino scrutiny.

FEWER DECKS

One of the easiest ways to improve our performance is to play where the fewest number of decks are in use. As we saw in Chapter 2, all else being equal, a game with fewer decks has a higher basic strategy expectation. This means that the disadvantage we have to overcome is smaller. Also, a game with fewer decks has greater fluctuations (in deck composition). Recall that the key to card counting is identifying favorable situations and taking advantage of them. These favorable situations arise when cards come out in "unexpected"

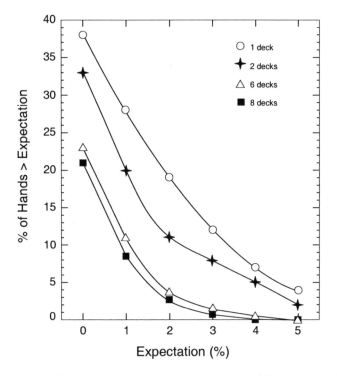

Figure 9: *The percentage of time that a game will afford the player a prescribed advantage. In a single-deck game, the player has an advantage nearly 40% of the time, dropping to about 20% in 8 decks.*

It's impossible to count multiple decks

BLACKJACK
Fallacy

We've heard this many times.

Even Telly Savalas lamented the "difficulty" in his *ABCs of Blackjack* video, commenting, "If it's more than two decks, hey, forget it!"

The myth is further propagated when card counting is characterized as being primarily a feat of memory.

For example, consider John Scarne's thoughts on the subject: "The most valuable natural aptitude a blackjack player can possess is the fairly rare faculty of remembering most of the previously exposed cards. The player who cannot do this has little or no chance of beating the bank in the long run."

In fact, it isn't any more difficult to count multiple decks than it is a single deck. We start at a different IRC based on the number of decks in play, but after that, the mechanics are all the same. We don't attempt to memorize the cards played.

It is, however, more difficult to *win* against multiple decks. As discussed earlier, the basic strategy expectation is lower, which means we have a greater hump to climb over. Furthermore, the favorable fluctuations in deck composition, hence the percentage of time when players have the advantage, are smaller. This means we'll have to use a larger betting spread in order to gain the same advantage.

So while the level of difficulty does not increase for counting multiple decks, we are often better off seeking out games with fewer decks.

proportions compared to the average, such that an excess of high cards remains. In games with fewer decks, this will occur more often.

A corollary to this is that a multiple-deck game requires a greater betting spread to yield the same profitability. Since the fluctuations in composition are less dramatic, the percentage of time that the player has the advantage goes down, making it necessary to bet more when these opportunities arise.

BETTER PENETRATION

Another way to improve results is to find better deck penetration. This means that more cards are dealt out prior to a shuffle, which means we are bound to be getting closer to the pivot point (our ultimate destiny if all the cards are dealt). Hence, there will be more times when we have the advantage.

As mentioned in the last chapter, don't worry that better penetration will render the strategy matrix numbers inaccurate. If you find a dealer who deals far into the pack, the gain in expectation (from additional volatility in the count closer to the pivot point) from more (and better) betting opportunities will far outweigh the tiny disadvantage inherited from diminished accuracy in strategic play.

FEWER PLAYERS

Playing with fewer or no other players at the table allows you to see more cards before making decisions. Indeed, if you're playing head-up with the dealer, you'll get to see all the cards as they're played with no problem. But there's a downside to head-up play: Some dealers are very fast. To a

That third-baseman is killing me

BLACKJACK
Fallacy

Can the play of another player, no matter how good or bad, affect your chances of winning at blackjack? Many people believe it can, that bad players somehow "bring down" an entire table with their poor plays. Not so.

In reality, the play of others has no impact on your own fortune. (The only exception to this is if the other players use all of the remaining cards, causing a re-shuffle.) If there are sufficient cards to finish the round, then other players have no overall effect on your expected outcome.

Let's take a mathematical look at why this is true. Say we know that the remaining deck contains x good cards (tens and aces), y bad cards (2s through 7s), and z neutral cards (8s and 9s).

At the end of the deck, the running count will be +4. So the present running count is $4 + x - y$. Now let's consider the next hit. The following are the probabilities of getting a good, bad, or neutral card:

$$P(x) = x/(x + y + z)$$
$$P(y) = y/(x + y + z)$$
$$P(z) = z/(x + y + z)$$

Assume for the moment that someone playing ahead of us takes a hit. If the player takes a good card, there are now only $(x - 1)$ good cards and $(x + y + z - 1)$ total cards remaining, so our chance of getting a good card after him would then be $(x - 1) / (x + y + z - 1)$. Likewise if the player gets a bad card, our chance of getting a good card would be $x / (x + y + z - 1)$. Finally, if the player gets a neutral card, our chance of getting a good card would again be $x / (x + y + z - 1)$. To determine our overall chance of getting a good card, we need to multiply each of these conditional chances by their respective probabilities, and add. This yields:

$$P(x) = \left[x/(x+y+z)\right] \times \left[(x-1)/(x+y+z-1)\right]$$

$$+\left[y/(x+y+z)\right] \times \left[x/(x+y+z-1)\right]$$

$$+\left[z/(x+y+z)\right] \times \left[x/(x+y+z-1)\right]$$

Collecting terms in the numerator gives us:

$$P(x) = x(x+y+z-1)/\left[(x+y+z)(x+y+z-1)\right]$$

or simply:

$$P(x) = x/(x+y+z)$$

And this, as you can see, is precisely the original chance of getting a good card if we had taken the first hit! It makes no difference whether an earlier player takes a hit, or two hits, or 20 hits. Overall, we still have the same chance of getting the card we want, as long as there's at least one card left after he's done with his hand. Furthermore, as long as sufficient cards are left to finish the round, it makes no difference how other players play, in terms of the expected final value of your hand or the dealer's hand, and hence, your chance of ultimately winning or losing.

novice counter this is often problematic, since in the rush you may find it difficult to keep the count and recall the correct plays. On the other hand, once you have the mechanics down cold, you'll find that head-up play is quick and allows you to wager more money in a given amount of time.

EXIT STRATEGY TO AVOID POOR COUNTS

We've discussed the technique of back-counting, which allows you to avoid poor counts. Let's apply the same concept in a different context. Say you're playing in a 2-deck game and one deck has already been dealt. The standard RC should now be near 0. If it's, say, –6 instead, your expectation is obviously negative. You may want to pick up your chips and find another table, rather than play out the last few hands. Or, you may want to take a well-timed lavatory break. With proper timing, you can get up, stretch your legs, hit the restroom, and return in time for the end of the shuffle and the start of a fresh deck, thus successfully avoiding playing in several hands with a probable negative expectation.

To this end, the K-O count can be played with an "exit strategy." An "exit condition" is a pair of numbers consisting of an exit count and an exit point. If you're at or below the exit count at the exit point, you leave the game. This is an advanced strategy that's most useful in shoe games.

For example, in the standard counting scheme, we start the K-O IRC at –20 for six decks or –28 for eight decks. The exit strategy consists of the following conditions.

Use the table entries (pg. 118) as follows. First locate the column corresponding to the game in question (6 or 8 decks). Then, determine the appropriate exit points from the left-most column.

Thus, in a 6-deck game, we can leave after 1 deck has been dealt if the running count is less than or equal to –22. So if we're playing at a 6-deck table and notice that 1/4 of the way through the shoe (1 1/2 decks dealt), the running count suddenly falls to –24, it's beneficial for us to exit the game. Similarly, in an 8-deck game, you can leave after playing 3 decks if the running count is less than or equal to –22, and so forth.

K-O STANDARD EXIT STRATEGY

	If RC ≤	
Leave	6-deck	8-deck
After 1 deck dealt	–22	–32
After 2 decks dealt	–17	–27
After 3 decks dealt	–12	–22
After 4 decks dealt	—	–17

Of course, adopting the exit strategy requires you to roughly estimate the number of decks already played. However, the deck estimation need not be too accurate: anything within 20% will do.

We can now introduce the exit strategy into the K-O Fabulous Fives 6-deck variation. Remember, we've shifted the IRC by +17, so we need to adjust the exit counts by the same amount. This leaves us with the following conditions for a 6-deck game: Leave at –5 or less after 1 deck is played; leave at 0 or less after 2 decks; and leave at +5 or less after 3 decks. Again, all values are divisible by 5.

The proper use of an exit strategy will nearly double your win-rate per hand. Not surprisingly, this is because you avoid situations with unfavorable conditions. The combination of a higher expectation coupled with a larger average bet size yields a tremendous gain in the win rate.

LONGEVITY

Since blackjack is one of the few casino games that's potentially beatable, casinos instruct pit personnel to watch for card counters. In principle, the pit can identify counters by counting the cards themselves. More often, though, they rely on other "tells" to determine if players are counting. To deflect this, good counters throw curves by acting naive, making erratic plays (known as "cover plays"), and otherwise behaving contrary to what's expected from the stereotypical nerdy counter. As such, the life of a card counter consists of an ongoing cat-and-mouse game with casino personnel. The card counter is attempting to portray himself as unworthy of attention, while the pit boss is looking for anyone who appears to be too proficient. Let's take a look at what we're up against.

The casino takes two primary steps in dealing with card counters: identification and action. In our opinion, counters should strive to avoid identification, since after they've been spotted, it's usually all she wrote. The most profitable time for a card counter is before he has been identified, or even suspected. After identifying you, the casino will take countermeasures to thwart your effectiveness.

Many pit supervisors actually do know how to count. This is not true of all of them, but even those who don't count are aware of certain clues, the tell-tale mannerisms that card counters typically exhibit, including large bet variation, efforts to see every card, and deep concentration. Other subtler tells include taking insurance only with a big bet out (there is a high correlation), never making a big bet off the top of a new deck, never drinking, and never tipping the dealer.

Because all card-counting systems require bet variation and strategy adjustments that are very similar, it really doesn't matter which particular system the player uses or the supervisor knows. If a casino boss is proficient and watches your play long enough, he will probably be able to tell whether or not you're counting.

For this reason, many counters "cool it" if the pit boss comes over to watch. They begin flat-betting (making the same bet regardless of the count) and in many cases revert to playing basic strategy only. This continues until the pit boss leaves to go hound another player. Unfortunately, it's hard (and unnatural) to be constantly on the lookout for floor personnel while playing; while one pit boss is leaving, there may be another right behind you still watching.

In some casinos, a suspicious pit boss may initiate countermeasures on his own. At other places, he may call a buddy over and they may both stare you down for a while. This "heat" is designed to unnerve card counters and is remarkably effective. At larger establishments, roving expert counters are sometimes employed and called upon to evaluate the skill of a player who is suspected by the pit. The expert may be brought into the pit to observe the player for 15 to 30 minutes before rendering judgment.

Other high-end casinos employ even more sophisticated means. There is now card-counting software that allows surveillance staff to input, by voice, a player's wagers, cards, and strategic decisions. The program then rates each player by estimating the player's expectation.

It's interesting to note that while many players "count," not all are good enough to actually derive a positive expectation. Errors in counting, coupled with errors in play and timidity in employing a large betting spread, often conspire to make good players not quite good enough to come out ahead in the long run.

Casinos also know this. A common theme we've found, in speaking with casino executives, is that while analyzing a potential card counter, the key point is to determine whether or not the player is good enough to *beat* the casino. The player may be counting cards, yet still be playing with an overall

THE ANNUAL BARGE "MASS BARRING"

The primary gaming family on the Internet is the rec.gambling newsgroup. Every August, members of rec.gambling descend on Las Vegas for the annual Big August Rec.Gambling Excursion, or BARGE.

BARGE members are clearly computer literate and generally knowledgeable in the field of blackjack. Many of them discuss the topic electronically on a daily basis. A sizable percentage of them are card counters.

It has become an unwritten ritual for a group of BARGErs to converge at a casino of choice for a traditional mass-barring. The mass-barring is typically a nonprofit event in which the intent is to get kicked out as quickly as possible, hoping to make a big scene for the gang in the process.

During BARGE '95, a group of us headed over to one of the smaller casinos on the Strip. Several BARGErs scattered to different tables, while some chose to enjoy the action from a vantage point at the bar. Our group found a $5 table with a lone player at 2nd base. Paul took 1st base, and Ubalanced Kid sat down next to him. Monte found an opening on the other side of the table at 3rd base. With two drinks in hand, Monte immediately clamored for a double vodka-something-or-other. We all cashed in for chips and started to play, betting $5 each.

The pit boss asked Monte if he would like to be rated, and Monte inaugurated the affair with the witty, if predictable, reply, "No, I really don't want a Big Mac for dinner." (At the time, the casino had a McDonald's on property.)

Shortly thereafter, the count went positive and Monte announced "plus three" while standing up and counting on his fingers. This was the cue for everyone to verbally verify his count level.

"Omega-II says plus six."

"I get five with K-O."

"High-Low gives three."

We all jumped our bets to $25 and Murph "wonged" in with $10 on the open spot next to Monte. The dealer's hands began to tremble. But she drew to a three-card 20 on the next round, wiping out the table. As fate would have it, the count climbed even higher.

At this point, both Paul and Monte jumped their bets to $100, while Murph and Kid each bet $25. The dealer dealt Paul his first card—the queen of clubs. That was enough to prompt the pit boss to rush to the table, push Paul's bet out of the circle, and say, "OK, you're through" (the first barring). He also pushed Monte's bet out (two down). He then touched Murph's bet but decided to leave it. He also ignored Kid's $25 bet. Apparently, it wouldn't look too good to bar the whole table.

Paul protested, rightfully perturbed at not being able to play his queen. But it was to no avail. Despite inheriting Paul's queen, Kid lost his hand anyway. Murph won his hand and picked up his chips.

Mission accomplished. Monte delivered a parting salvo as he politely asked for his comp to McDonald's. Everyone tried to keep straight faces as the pit boss, not surprisingly, ignored him.

Meanwhile. . .

As our table was attracting all sorts of attention, two other BARGErs known as Geoff and Bozo used the misdirection to good result at another table. They were able to play for more than an hour, spreading from $5 to $100 and amassing a profit of nearly $1,000 before finally getting the boot.

negative expectation. If the bosses decide that a player is not capable enough to pose a threat, the house may still deal to the player. (Strangely enough, some professional blackjack players seem to almost *need* to be barred every so often—to validate their skills.)

To most, being barred is not an enjoyable experience. The reality that the "enemy" has now discovered you unnerves many counters. If you are barred (or just asked to leave), pick up all of your money and chips; these are yours. Don't just leave the table; leave the casino, too. In Nevada, casinos are still allowed to refuse the action of players who are "too good." This is no longer true in Atlantic City.

While technology today can assist the casino in identifying card counters, it's still too labor intensive to track everyone in this fashion. Thus, it's still typically left to the floorman to first suspect someone of counting, which, in turn, sets off the chain of events. The key to longevity, then, is to avoid this first pressure point. If possible, you should disguise your counting from the pit personnel.

CASINO COUNTERMEASURES

After identifying a card counter, the casino has several options. In terms of altering the game procedures, the house can take action in several ways (all detrimental to the card counter).

Probably foremost, the house can shuffle earlier in the pack. As the penetration is decreased, the card counter faces a progressively steep uphill climb. Recall that deep penetration into the pack is desirable for card counters.

Another countermeasure is to restrict a player to flat betting. Clearly, a betting spread of some sort is required for a card counter to be successful, and if a casino imposes flat betting, this is bad news for your card-counting career at this establishment.[40]

A casino can also introduce more decks into the game. Remember, fewer decks are preferable for players.

The house may resort to preferential shuffling, which means the dealer shuffles at will. In its worst form, a floorman or dealer counts down the deck and preferentially shuffles the pack when the count becomes favorable to the player. In our opinion, this is unethical, as it changes the expectation for the game even for players who are not counting, and hence, are oblivious to what is happening to them.

The casino may also change the actual rules of the game. This can be anything from more restrictive doubling to disallowing insurance. The house might even close the table to get a counter to move to one that's more crowded.

Once this starts happening, there isn't much point in sticking around. If you challenge them just to prove that you can still beat their game, the casino will eventually construct a game that is unbeatable. And the longer you play, the more likely you are to be recognized the next time around.

In our opinion, you're past the point of no return once the pit has an inkling that you're a counter; it's only a matter of time before countermeasures will be employed, and you'll be left with a game that is unprofitable.

WHAT TO DO?

This is the major question facing card counters. The answer is to develop an "act" of some sort. That is, learn to

---

[40] For a technique known as "depth-charging," in which bet spreading is not required, see Snyder's *Blackbelt in Blackjack*. The technique makes use of the added strategic benefits of card counting, but is successful only in single-deck games in which the player can sit at third base and see all the cards that have been played.

MIT INTERNATIONAL ESCAPADES

Though card-counting is *not* illegal in the United States, some foreign countries look upon the matter differently. Also, casinos in foreign lands may purchase secret information about card counters from American casino detective agencies.

Consider Andy, Semyon, and Katie, members of the famous MIT blackjack team, revered by players and feared by the casinos. The three were applying their skills in Monte Carlo, well known for gaming resorts, auto races, and Grace Kelly.

Now it just so happened that Semyon was listed in the "Griffin Book," a compilation of "known" card counters and/or card cheats (it would be more accurate to describe the book as a compilation of "suspected" offenders).

After winning quite a bit of money, the trio was escorted into a back room, where they were held for more than an hour and their pictures were taken. Then a Monte Carlo police inspector walked in.

The team spent the next five hours in the custody of the cops. The police searched their rental car and questioned all three individually. Semyon received a particularly long and probing interrogation since he was in the Griffin book. He was told that card-counting was illegal in Monte Carlo.

However, the team was never charged with committing any crime (and was allowed to keep their winnings). After a couple more hours of detention, they were finally allowed to leave, with instructions to get in their car and not return to Monte Carlo. In keeping with the regal treatment afforded by the authorities, they received a police escort all the way to the border.

disguise your play.

The life expectancy of a card counter can be considerably extended with the use of a good act. What's more, we've found that the implementation of the act can be the most enjoyable part of the game. The Knock-Out system's ease of use allows players more time and energy to concentrate on laying the "camouflage" that's sometimes necessary to play skilled blackjack in a casino environment.

Being allowed to ply your newfound card-counting skills is an important consideration, and one that's been tackled in different ways by different authors. Here is a sampling:

The late Ken Uston[41] was a former vice president of the Pacific Stock Exchange and the best-selling author of a book on, of all things, the video game Pac-Man. In the blackjack world, Uston was the man responsible for Atlantic City's law that disallows the banning of card counters. Uston also tried to have the practice outlawed in Nevada, though unsuccessfully.

While playing in a casino, Uston would often appear flat-out drunk. He would mumble incoherently and teeter precariously on his seat in order to convince the pit that he was unworthy of attention. Once his act succeeded, he was able to employ enormous bet spreads. However, no act is perfect, and after Uston was identified and barred from several establishments, he was forced to resort to elaborate physical disguises to continue playing.

In one amusing incident, Uston pulled a stunt on his card-counting buddies while at the Dunes. While playing in a situation with an exceptionally high count, Uston put a pair of underpants on his head, on which were emblazoned, "I crapped out in Vegas." He bet $500 and won the wager. Then, to the astonishment of all, he threw his "hat" on the layout,

---

[41] See *Million Dollar Blackjack* or *Ken Uston on Blackjack*.

tossed his cash and chips over to another player at the table, and ran out of the casino. The stunned casino bosses didn't know that the player who was thrown the chips was actually one of Uston's partners. The escapade branded him as a lunatic whose play would be welcomed at the Dunes for years to come.

Later in his card-counting career, Uston formed teams that used the now-legendary "big player" (BP) technique. Big players can be used in several ways. In one common approach, little players are stationed at several tables in a casino, counting through the shoes and placing table-minimum bets while the BP wanders around aimlessly. Every so often, as superstitious high-rollers tend to do, the BP gets a "hunch" and plays a few hands, perhaps at the betting maximum, at a table chosen seemingly at random. Unbeknownst to casino personnel, the BP has actually been signaled into the game by one of the little players after the count has gone favorable.

When the BP arrives at the table, the present count may be relayed to him via signals worked out beforehand. Alternatively, the little player can simply make all betting and strategic decisions for the BP, again through signals. In this case, the BP need not know anything about expert play, only how to read and follow the signals. When the deck goes sour, the BP is signaled to leave. The BP then dawdles while waiting for the next signal indicating a juicy deck.

The beauty of this technique is that the BP makes only large wagers and always in positive situations. Because he never varies his bets, the BP appears to be a fun-loving high-roller, "haphazardly" making his way from one "lucky" table to the next. Casino personnel see a big bettor jumping from game to game, never staying at a particular table long enough to possibly be counting cards.

In a second technique, a little player and BP play together full-time at the same table. The little player usually flat bets a modest amount, while the BP bets much more, relying on the little player for all decisions. Again, this is all done via signals worked out beforehand.

In this second variation, the ploy is in the BP acting in a manner that makes it impossible for him (or her) to be counting cards. He can do whatever he wishes, and usually does. He'll look up at the mirrored ceiling, check out the cocktail waitresses, tie his shoes, talk sports with the pit bosses, go to the bathroom, whatever, because his associate is counting the cards for him and telling him exactly how to proceed at all times. Indeed, some teams have the BP simply play basic strategy throughout, leaving the gain to be realized from a large bet spread. The information about how much to bet is often relayed through the location (not amount) of the little player's wagers.[42]

Uston wrote of another incident in which one of his BPs had just lost a big double down at the Tropicana. "He grunted loudly, waved his arms, and knocked over his Bloody Mary. The table, cards, and chips were soaked with ice, booze, tomato juice, and pieces of lime. The dealer grabbed a towel. A boss ran over with new decks of cards." In the meantime, Uston's BP had noticed a teammate who was signaling him to an adjacent table. He stood up and left, commenting "I don't play at wet tables."

Ian Andersen[43] employs a solitary act to which he is well suited. He goes so far as to befriend dealers and pit personnel, all the while maintaining an air of humility as he feigns ignorance of the game. With well-placed gifts to the floormen and tips for the dealers, Andersen describes case after case where casino personnel have bent over backward to come to his aid.

In one fantastic story, a free-spirited casino executive

---

[42] Clearly this is not optimal, but recall that most of the advantage from card counting comes from proper betting decisions, not playing decisions.

[43] See *Turning the Tables on Las Vegas*, 1976, Vintage Books.

began "selling" information during a blackjack game. During the course of the session, much wheeling and dealing transpired between Andersen and this executive, who was a casino vice-president.

For starters, the VP offered Andersen the option to surrender a quarter of his bet without looking at his cards. Andersen, sensing that bigger things were to come, agreed and coughed up nearly $25. Apparently thinking he'd lured the biggest fish in the desert, the VP pressed on, "Tell you what. You can give me a quarter of your chips now and not play another hand." Andersen parried the thrust, "Nah, you'd be cheating yourself out of three-quarters of my chips." Shortly thereafter, Andersen was allowed to surrender a 16 vs. a dealer 10 for only one-eighth of his bet, saving several hundred dollars. On a subsequent hand, the VP freely turned over the dealer's hole card so that Andersen could decide how to play. Still later, Andersen had a $1,000 bet out and held two tens. The dealer's upcard was a 6, and Andersen again inquired whether he would be allowed see the dealer's hole card. This time there was a "fee" of $200. It was well worth it, as the downcard was a 10. Knowing the dealer had 16, Andersen proceeded to split and resplit his tens a total of five times, winding up with totals of 14, 16, 21, 19, 15, and 18. The dealer hit his hand with a 7 and busted. Less the $200 "investment," Andersen won $6,000.

Indeed, in a new book, *Burning the Tables in Las Vegas*,[44] Andersen advocates "a complete paradigm shift," by which the player abandons the traditional adversarial stance with casino bosses in favor of a kinder, gentler, friendlier approach.

Lance Humble[45] adopted a much more conservative style

---

[44] *Burning the Tables in Las Vegas*, 1999, Huntington Press, provides the most exhaustive treatment of cover play ever written.

[45] See *The World's Greatest Blackjack Book*.

of play, in which he tried to avoid casino personnel altogether. A psychology professor, Humble recommends a method of play by which "you should avoid any unusual behavior in the casino." Everything from the way you hold your cards to the way you dress should fit right in. When it comes to methodically doubling and halving wagers for purposes of cover, Humble says, "This will reduce your advantage slightly from not responding immediately to a change in count, but these methods will help you to win in blessed anonymity."

Stanford Wong[46] has also weighed in on the subject. Wong points out that pit personnel see thousands of faces on a daily basis, and to remember undesirables, they tend to focus on peculiar attributes that they then associate with those players. So, Wong advises, "You need to have some outstanding feature that's under your control." In this vein, Wong has at times worn distinctive items of clothing and jewelry, acted intoxicated, and even appeared to have physical impediments. Then, if he's drawn heat on a previous visit, he can reappear at the casino without the feature, making it difficult for casino personnel to make the connection.

Wong has also long advocated the use of back-counting (or wonging as it has come to be affectionately called) to get maximum bang for your buck. You may recall that back-counting entails standing behind a game and counting down a pack. If it becomes favorable, you sit down and play. If it later becomes unfavorable, you get up and leave. In this way you avoid playing with a negative expectation. When you sit down, you must appear to have just begun playing (if properly done, the casino will not realize that you have picked your spot). You can throw out a big bet knowing that you have an advantage, and the casino will likely think that this is your average wager. You can maintain the big bets as long as

---

[46] See also Stanford Wong's *Blackjack Secrets*, 1994, Pi Yee Press.

the count remains sufficiently positive.

But back-counting is not without its problems. First, it's not that easy to stand behind a game and count down a deck. The main problem is that the players block your view. You must be strategically located so you can see all the cards.

It helps to have something to do while back-counting. You won't get away with it for long if, for an entire afternoon, all you do is stand behind table after table waiting to jump in. The bosses will eventually catch on to what you're doing and put a stop to it.

One good ruse is to pretend to be watching a sporting event on TV. Many casinos have TVs located on or near the casino floor. Find a table, or group of tables, located near some of the screens. In this way, you can watch the game, periodically glance down at the table to count the cards, and look back up at the TV to again pick up the action. If done with a drink or perhaps a newspaper sports section in hand, this can be milked for good effect.

Or you can pretend to be waiting for someone. It's not hard to make it appear as if you're looking for someone. Just look off into the distance as you approach a table. Frown, check your watch. Look around some more. Periodically glance at the table to keep the count. What's that? The count is now +4? "Well, I may as well play a few hands while I'm waiting," you can announce. To add credibility and give yourself some breathing room, have the floorman page your party. When the deck goes sour, get up and go, since you're already "late." Do it again in the casino next door.

Arnold Snyder has some interesting insights into playing the game. With one technique he calls "depth-charging,"[47] single-deck players can gain an advantage without using a betting spread. The key is deep deck penetration. As a dealer

---

[47] See *Blackbelt in Blackjack*.

goes deeper into the deck, the additional information on deck composition can be used to properly vary from basic strategic on enough occasions to gain an advantage. So, says Snyder, "The player always bets more deep in the deck, even when his count is negative. His playing strategy is so much more effective deep in the deck that he obtains a significant edge over the house." To take advantage of depth-charging, a system with a high "playing efficiency" must be used. Therefore, do not use depth-charging with the K-O system (recall that most of K-O's gain comes from proper betting variation).

A multiple-deck betting term coined by Snyder is "opposition betting," a concept credited to Ralph Stricker. Basically, opposition betting is a decoy maneuver designed to fool the pit personnel. Clearly, if the count is low, we want to bet only a little, and if the count is high we want to bet a lot. The middle ground is the fertile area for opposition play. During intermediate counts (when neither the casino nor player has a large advantage), you may wish to bet in an unpredictable manner, sometimes even *opposite* to the indication of the count.

For example, let's say we're playing an 8-deck shoe. The key count is –6. Now, for counts between roughly –9 and –3, the player's expectation falls between –0.5% and +0.5%. On hands played while the count is in this "opposition" range, you have an overall average expectation of about 0%. Thus, during this time, it's okay to haphazardly make bets with little rhyme or reason, knowing that overall you will come out about even.

Opposition plays should be made with the understanding that if the count rises out of the range, you will make a max bet much greater than any of the opposition wagers. Similarly, if the count falls below the range, you will make a minimum bet much smaller than the opposition wagers. Overall then, you're betting small with a disadvantage, haphazardly medium when you're roughly even, and large with an advantage—which is the whole point of card counting.

One counter we know has been successful with a different type of approach. When he plays, he acts like a blackjack novice who is in town for a good time. He'll nurse a drink while chatting and asking advice from neighbors, dealers, and floorpeople. He may even invite the pit boss over for his say. After the resolution of a losing hand, he'll make a comment designed to gently poke fun at the errant advice. Not enough to make the bosses mad, but enough so that they're a bit embarrassed and might think twice before coming back to the table. The key to this approach is to be good natured about the whole thing. If the pit's advice works, you might offer the fellow a tip or a drink. He has to decline, but offering a present such as this does several things.

First, a seasoned blackjack veteran would never offer the pit boss an outright monetary tip or alcoholic beverage while the boss is on duty. So making the gesture reassures the pit that you are a relative neophyte.

It also reinforces the fact that you're loose with your money. Card counters, as a rule, do not tip. That you're a tipper may make the boss think that you're an ordinary tourist bent on spreading the wealth.

Finally, your gracious act will also help keep the pit personnel at bay. After being offered a tip in plain sight of all at the table (and the eye-in-the-sky), the floorman figures to be slightly hesitant to come to your table again. Like most employees, he wants to avoid any actions that might look improper.

Again, though, the key is to act natural. You can't be a stoic robot as you watch the turn of every card. Show some emotion! That's what the rest of the players do. Thank the dealer for "giving" you a blackjack. Thank the third baseman for standing and "letting" the dealer have the bust card. The more superstitions you seem to believe, the more comfort-

ANOTHER CAT-AND-MOUSE GAME

In card counting, the cat-and-mouse game works both ways. Take the following example of casino infiltration into a card-counting school outside of Atlantic City.

Rich Tesler is the casino manager at Foxwoods, the world's largest casino. A casino floorman at the time, Rich and a colleague named Bob were dispatched to a local school to learn what they could about a new blackjack system. The four-week course cost $400 per person and consisted of two weeks of school study followed by two weeks of training in local casinos.

Bob arrived first in flashy garb, followed later by Rich dressed in a T-shirt and khaki pants. Their money was accepted. Soon the time came for all prospective students to introduce themselves. Bob volunteered that he was a professional player who preferred playing in the Bahamas, and was there to explore recent developments in blackjack. Rich was one of the last to speak, "I'm a carpenter who goes to Atlantic City once a week. I'm not a card counter, and I'm tired of getting my brains bashed in."

A short time later, Bob was invited into a back room and sent packing with his $400. His giveaway was the preference for Bahamian blackjack; no pro would try to buck this inferior game. The instructor, now on his guard, asked, "Are there any other new students?"

His wife replied, "The only new starter is Rich, but he's okay." How did she know? She'd noticed that Rich's money was wet. Rich had taken the time to pass his bills under running water before coming to class, reasoning that, "If I worked outside all day, then the bills in my pocket ought to be damp." It worked; Rich was allowed to stay.

able the pit personel will be having you play their game. Internally though, you must maintain a coldly logical approach.

Unfortunately, losses do occur—even while counting. Just as you aren't sure to lose every session while playing a negative-expectation game like roulette, you aren't sure to win every session of blackjack, despite your positive expectation.

We can cite countless examples of isolated incidents in which the results seem to defy all reason.

One expert player tells of an occasion on which he bought in for 20 units. On the next 20 hands, he lost 19 outright and split once—losing one of the split hands and pushing the other. Ouch! All the while an elderly lady at the table stood on all hard 14s, 15s, and 16s and was winning. Short-run fluctuations are inevitable; you simply can't read too much into the results from any particular session.

On another occasion, a fine fellow was back-counting a double-deck game when the count shot up to +8. He sat down and bet $25. There were two other players, and each received naturals while he was dealt a stiff and busted. A new player sat down. The count was still high so our man pushed out another $25. Bang, two more player blackjacks, but neither of them to him. Again he had a stiff, but this time didn't have to bust because the dealer had a natural, too. In just two rounds, five blackjacks had been dealt to a total of nine hands. In a freshly shuffled double-deck game, the chances of this happening are about 1 in 150,000. Unfortunately, the only card counter at the table didn't participate in the fun.

In another oddball hand, while playing third base in another double-deck game on the Strip, this same player had a count of +6. He was feeling pretty good about his chances. That feeling subsided a bit when he was dealt 16. The dealer had an ace up, which didn't help his feelings either. As required by the K-O system (remember the new running count is now +5 including the 10,6 and the dealer's ace), he took insurance and promptly lost it. Hmmm. When his turn came,

---

COUNTING BY SOUND

Everyone knows the way to count is by sight, right? Not necessarily.

A subtle way to get the job done is to find dealers who *mention* the values of the cards as they're played. This occurs almost exclusively in shoe games (and mainly on the East Coast) where all cards are typically dealt face-up on the table. Many dealers will assist patrons by announcing their totals following hits.

For example, if you see that a player has a total of 10 before hitting, and then *hear* the dealer say that his new total is 16 after the hit, you know that the card was a 6, and has a card-counting value of +1. You can actually turn away from the table, apparently not interested in the outcome of the other hands, while maintaining the count all along.

The best way to make use of this technique is to first locate such a dealer. The best kind is one who announces each player's total after the first two cards, then again after every hit. First count the value of the cards initially dealt to the players. You may now be able to direct your attention away from the table (look for a cocktail waitress, chat while facing the pit boss, etc.), mentally keeping track of the count based on the dealer's announcements. It takes a while to get the hang of it, but counting by sound is a lot of fun, and good cover when done correctly.

---

he hit and immediately busted. What transpired next added insult to injury. The count was still quite high as the dealer began to play out his hand. First, he flipped over his hole card—an ace (bing...). Next he took a hit—another ace (bang…). He motioned to his arriving replacement dealer to take a gander; he now held a soft 13. The next hit—another ace (boom). The hand now consisted of four aces! With this the floorman had to be called over to witness the dealer's prowess. The next hit was a ten (unbelievable, the dealer's hand of five cards now had a net running count of –5). With a hard 14, the next hit was a 2, for a total of 16. Would the dealer go by the wayside, as our hero had only a few seconds earlier? The next hit was a 5, completing the 7-card 21. Hands like these clear out tables pretty quickly.

Even in the midst of long losing streaks, you can take solace in knowing that you're playing correctly. If the count is high, you should expect to see an excess of aces and tens appear. If they do, even if you don't get them, you should feel a little better knowing that you're correctly keeping track of the game.

OTHER IDEAS

Some counters subscribe to a maximum-damage *commando* type of philosophy. In this Arnold Schwarzenegger frame of mind, the counter goes in knowing he will play only, perhaps, 30 minutes, then leave. The idea is to go in with reckless abandon concerning his bet spread. Sure, the casino will eventually pick up on what he's doing, but hopefully he'll be gone by then. This technique is obviously not recommended if playing in an area with only a few casinos, since you'll soon run out of places to play.

Another technique sometimes employed is "steaming." Steaming means pretending to be so emotionally charged up in the game that you can't control your wagering. It works well for getting more money on the table when the count is very high. The idea is to pretend to be so flustered that you start to lose control, wagering more and more.

Let's say the count is high and you make a correspondingly large wager of $100. You lose the hand. Muttering and cursing to yourself you reach into your pocket and pull out $200 in cash. Rather than bet a portion, you throw it down in an apparent attempt to get the first $100 back. You lose again, but the count is even higher. You act incensed; your hands start to shake a little as you reach in and grab another wad of bills. How much? Nobody knows. You throw it down and angrily say, "Bet it all." Mission accomplished. Win or lose, you've just managed to continually increase your wager in a favorable situation.

Steaming can often be used to good advantage near the end of a pack just before the shuffle. If a pit boss suspects you're on tilt, he may instruct the dealer to go ahead and deal another round rather than risk your regaining your senses during the two minutes the dealer is shuffling. Steamers generally have to leave when the dealer does finally shuffle since the advantage is gone.

Tipping, or "toking" as the dealers call it, is a subject that doesn't receive too much attention in most blackjack books. On the face of it, tipping has an expectation of -100%. If you tip, that money is lost. For most card counters, this rules out tipping completely.

But beneath the surface, it's not always true that tipping is worthless, and indeed in some instances, tipping may have value. Certainly if you want to look like a tourist who's in town for a good time, it would not be unreasonable to make tipping a part of your act. It may allow you to play longer without any heat from the pit.

Some players try to use tipping to increase deck penetration. It's our opinion that tipping for this purpose in shoe games is not usually effective. If a tip causes the dealer to act on your behalf (place the cut card lower in the shoe) at all, the small gain will probably not make up for the cost of the tip.

In hand-held games, on the other hand, the dealer will

often not use a cut-card to indicate a shuffle point. Rather, he will estimate the number of remaining cards before deciding whether or not to deal another round. In cases such as these, a few well-timed tips may get you better penetration in situations where it will do you some good.

Furthermore, in games in which the dealer "peeks" by manually checking[48] the hole card under aces and/or tens, tipping may also gain you additional information. The dealer, if rooting for you, may subtly help you during the course of the game. For example, he may, if holding a stiff, quickly pass you by if you're wavering between hitting or standing on your own stiff. The rationale is that the more you win, the more tips he'll get.

With juicy counts near the shuffle point, a toke sometimes persuades the dealer to deal one more round. These "specific tokes," as Arnold Snyder has labeled them, must be dispensed with great care. Even with a K-O running count of +4 (the pivot point, so roughly a 2% advantage), a $5 tip on a $50 hand will cost you 10%, leading to a large overall negative expectation for the hand.

Be aware, also, that collusion with the dealer is a definite no-no. We do not advocate cheating of any type; we only make the point that tipping is not necessarily a total waste of money. After all, dealers are human, despite what others may tell you.

Cover plays are an interesting camouflage idea. Cover plays are typically either bets or plays made at incorrect times. For example, with a running count of +4, we'd like to make a big bet. However, if the pit boss is breathing down our neck, the large wager might be our last. Under these conditions, it

---

[48] This should not be confused with the automated or mirrored "peek" mechanisms now in place at many casinos. With these mechanical instruments, the dealer has the same information as the player, namely whether or not he has a natural.

might be appropriate to make a cover bet of a single unit. The play is made to throw off the pit personnel in case they too are counting the game.

Another popular cover play is to make a big wager right after the shuffle. Even if the pit personnel are not counting, they know that a player has no advantage off the top in a freshly shuffled game. So making a big bet at this point is a way for a card counter to say, "Look, the count means nothing to me."

Still other cover plays involve the actual play of the hand. Every once in a while, hopefully with a small bet out, you may want to make a slightly incorrect play. This should be done only if you know that someone is analyzing your play. And even in this case it should not be overdone, as every incorrect play costs you money.[49]

Overall, you need to stick to the game plan. Any deviation from it costs money. If you insist on making frequent cover plays, then you will not be successful. It's time to work on your overall act.

WARNING TO BEGINNERS

If you're diligent, you'll get to the point where you can play the Knock-Out system and almost never make an error—on your kitchen table, that is. Playing in a casino is a different story, unlike any other experience you're likely to encounter. Casinos are full of distractions: bright lights, cocktail waitresses, drinks, clattering chips, other gamblers talking (or cheering), pit bosses, dealers, you name it. When attempting to count cards for the first time in a casino environment, you're bound to make some mistakes. Even if you play perfectly

---

[49] This is the primary theme in Andersen's *Burning the Tables in Las Vegas*.

while practicing at home, being under the gun in a casino is something else altogether. There's no substitute for experience, and you'll get better in real conditions as you go. But in the meantime, here are a few simple rules to follow that will help you through your first blackjack card-counting session:

1) Bet the table minimum until you're comfortable with your counting. That is, count cards and mentally note the correct plays, but bet the table minimum until you're confident of your abilities. It may take an hour or more to become accustomed to the surroundings.

2) If you lose the count during play, bet the table minimum until the next shuffle. Recall that you'll always start the count at the IRC after a shuffle.

3) If you're losing, don't start betting more money to "try to get it all back at once" (this might be a good time to reread Chapter 7 on the care that must be taken when betting). Remember, a card counter bets more only when he has a mathematical advantage. However, it seems to be a part of human nature, when losing, to want to bet more money in an effort to recoup your losses as quickly as possible. This often leads to even greater losses. All card counters have both winning and losing sessions. Keep the big picture in mind: In the long run, our advantage will bear out, and the long run is made up of countless sessions. Don't let short-run fluctuations get the best of you, whether monetarily or psychologically.

SUMMARY

• Several methods to enhance profits are available to card counters. Seeking out better playing conditions, employing more sophisticated betting techniques and/or exit strategies, or using an act can all be fruitful. But tipping and cover plays eat away at profits and should not be overused.

• Donald Schlesinger provides perhaps the best summary for this chapter when he says, "The goal is to walk into a casino and win the most money possible, consistent with being welcomed back the next time."

• As a synopsis, we present a final "Top 10" list:

TOP 10 PHRASES CARD COUNTERS
SHOULD NEVER SAY AT THE BLACKJACK TABLE

10. "What's the count?"
9. "Can I sit out a few hands while the low cards come out?"
8. "Uhh. . . ma'am. I can't keep up when you scoop up the cards so fast."
7. "Do you give good penetration?"
6. "I just finished reading *Knock-Out Blackjack*. Is this the DOA, DAS, S17, table that allows back-counting and mid-shoe entry?"
5. "Go ahead and deal another round! You won't run out of cards. It's mostly tens and aces left."
4. "My name? Thorp. Dr. Edward O. Thorp."
3. "Yeah. Like I'm gonna take even money with a count of −7."
2. "Please tell the first-baseman to hold his cards so I can see them."
1. "Zero, plus one, plus two, plus one, zero, minus one, minus two..."

Appendix

Appendix I: Rules of Blackjack

Blackjack is played at a semicircular table, where typically up to seven players can play at once. The game is usually played with 1, 2, 6, or 8 standard 52-card decks. We shall refer to the totality of cards (whether a single deck or eight decks or anything in between) as the *pack*.

The total value of a hand is the sum of the individual cards making up the hand. Each card is worth its face value, and suits are irrelevant. Face-value cards all count as 10. Aces can be counted as either 1 or 11.

Blackjack gets its name because a blackjack, or *natural*, is the best possible hand. A natural is a total of 21 on the first two cards. This can be achieved only by being dealt an ace and any ten (10, jack, queen, or king).

To begin play, each player makes a wager in the betting circle in front of him. The dealer first deals every player a card, then deals himself a card face up. He then deals every player a second card, and his own second card face down.

If the dealer's upcard is an ace, *insurance* is offered. This is an optional side bet; players so inclined may wager up to one-half their original wager on insurance. If the dealer has the natural, then the insurance bet wins and is paid 2 to 1, after which the main hands are then settled. If the dealer does not have a natural, the insurance bet is lost, and play continues in the usual fashion.

With a ten upcard, the dealer will also check, via manual

or mechanical means, to see if he has a natural (an ace as the hole card).[50] If the dealer has a natural, all players' hands lose (unless a player also has a natural, in which case that player pushes with the dealer). If the dealer does not have a natural, play continues in the usual fashion.

If the dealer has any other value upcard (or has an upcard of ace or ten but does not have a natural), play continues. In turn, each player finishes the play of his hand before the dealer goes on to the next player. The player to the dealer's immediate left, commonly referred to as the *first base position*, acts first.

This player has several options based on the value of his first two cards: *hit, stand, double down, split,* or *surrender*.

Hitting: After looking at his original two cards, the player may wish to draw another card. If so, he will tap the table near his cards, signaling he wants to hit.[51] The dealer will deal him another card, face up, in front of his wager. The player's new total is now the sum of the three cards. The player may continue to hit as long as his total does not exceed 21. If the player goes over a total of 21, he has *busted* and immediately loses his wager.

Standing: If the player is satisfied with his hand and has not busted, he may elect to stand. He does this by waving his hand, palm down, over the wager.[52]

---

[50] Some casinos will not check under the ten. After all players have completed their hands, the dealer will turn over the hole card. If the dealer has a natural, usually only original player wagers are at risk. Check with the dealer if in doubt.

[51] In hand-held games, players scratch the table with their cards to indicate hitting.

[52] In hand-held games, players slide the original two cards under the wager to indicate standing.

Doubling down: In most casinos in the United States, a player may double down on any first two cards.[53] To double down, a player places another wager, less than or equal to the original, alongside the original bet. The player then receives one and only one additional card, regardless of its value. The hands are resolved in the usual fashion, and the payoffs are based on the new total wager.

Splitting: If the player's two original cards have the same value (e.g., 7,7 or 10,K), he may elect to split the hand. To do so, he places an equal wager alongside the original. The player then plays two separate hands, with one original card providing the first card of each new hand. Standard hitting and standing rules apply, except for split aces, on which you may draw only one card each. Furthermore, if the next card to a split ace is a ten, the hand's value is 21 but is not considered a natural. Resplitting and doubling down after the original split are subject to the rules of the house.

Surrendering: Some casinos offer the surrender option, in which, after seeing his first two cards, a player may end the hand (without playing further) by giving up half of the original wager. Of those American casinos that have the surrender option, most offer only *late surrender*, which allows the option only if the dealer doesn't have a natural.

If you are allowed to surrender your hand before the dealer checks his hole card for a natural, it's called *early surrender*. Early surrender is rare because it's very valuable for the player (worth about .63%). If you encounter this option, early surrender hard 5-7 and hard 12-17 vs. A; hard 14-16 vs. ten; and hard 16 (except split 8,8) vs. 9.

After all players have finished playing their hands, it is

---

[53] See Chapter 2 for a discussion of more restrictive doubling rules.

the dealer's turn. The dealer makes no subjective decisions and plays his hand according to a fixed set of rules. In most of the United States, the dealer must hit until either reaching a *pat* total of 17 through 21 or busting.[54]

If the dealer busts, all players who have not previously busted, regardless of the value of their hands, are paid 1 to 1. If the dealer has not busted, the value of the dealer's hand is compared to that of every player still in the game. If the player's total is higher, the player is paid 1 to 1. If the totals are equal, the hand is a push. If the dealer's total is greater, the player's wager is lost. All bets are resolved at this time, then new bets are made, and the whole sequence starts over.

---

[54] See Chapter 2 for a discussion of the alternative, where the dealer hits soft 17.

Appendix II: Blackjack Jargon

Back-Counting: A method of card-counting while not playing, first proposed by Ed Thorp and popularized by Stanford Wong. Often standing in back of the seated players, the back-counter will begin playing only when the deck becomes favorable.

Balanced System: A card-counting system in which the sum of the card values is equal to zero. A true-count conversion is required for betting and playing decisions.

Bust: To obtain a hard total greater than 21.

Cutoff: Number of cards to be left unplayed, often delineated by a cut-card. See also "penetration."

Dealer: Individual who represents the house and is responsible for dealing the cards, determining the outcome of the game, and settling wagers.

Downcard: The dealer's face-down card, also referred to as the hole card.

First Base: The position immediately to the dealer's left. A player seated at first base acts first.

Floorman: Individual responsible for overseeing a group of several blackjack tables. Subordinates include dealers.

Hard Hand: Any hand totaling 12 or more in which there is either no ace or all aces are counted as 1.

Level: In a point-count system, the maximum of the absolute values of integers assigned to respective cards. For example, a system employing a range of values from -3 to +2 would be a level-3 system.

Natural: A two-card total of 21 on the initial hand, also referred to as a blackjack.

Pack: The set of cards in play; for example an 8-deck shoe game uses a pack of 416 cards.

Pat: Any total of 17 through 21.

Penetration: The percentage of total cards that are dealt. For example, a dealer who cuts off 2 decks in an 8-deck shoe game yields a penetration of 75%.

Pit: A ring-like arrangement of casino gaming tables, where patrons typically wager from the outside and casino personnel are situated in the interior.

Pit Boss: Individual responsible for overseeing an entire pit. Subordinates include floormen and dealers.

Push: A tie.

Shoe: Plastic box used to hold and deal multiple decks.

Side Count: An additional count (e.g., of aces) that is kept in conjunction with the main count.

Soft Hand: Any hand containing an ace in which the ace is counted as 11.

Stiff: Any hard total of 12 through 16.

Ten: A card with a value of 10, i.e., 10, jack, queen, or king.

Third Base: The position immediately to the dealer's right. A player seated at third base acts last.

Type: The category of a point-count card-counting system, either balanced or unbalanced.

Unbalanced System: A card-counting system in which the sum of the card values is not equal to zero. No true-count conversion is necessary.

Upcard: The dealer's face-up card.

Wonging: See "back-counting." ⸺

Appendix III: A Comparison of the K-O System to Other Sytems

Here we take a look at some of the other popular card-counting systems to see how K-O measures up. You'll see that the lean K-O system holds its own against all the "heavyweights" with their extra baggage of multiple-level counts, side counts, and/or true-count conversions.

Ease of Use

The unbalanced nature of the Knock-Out count (which eliminates the need for estimation of remaining decks and a true-count conversion), the natural level-1 card values, the absence of any side counts, the innovation of a reduced and rounded matrix, and the flexibility for customization make the K-O system unique. To date, no other system has all of these attributes.

System Comparison: Ease of Use

System	Type	Level	Side count?	Round matrix?
K-O	U	1	N	Y
Red 7	U	1+*	N	N
UZ II	U	2	N	N
Hi-Opt I	B	1	Y	N
High-Low	B	1	N	N
Omega II	B	2	Y	N

*Red 7 requires the player to keep track of colors on 7-valued cards.

The table on the preceding page compares the most popular systems today in terms of ease of use. The first three comparison parameters (type, level, and whether or not a side count is employed) are intrinsic properties for each particular system and are, therefore, fixed.[55]

The comparison parameter to the far right (whether or not a rounded matrix exists) is included for the present-day version of these systems. In principle, any system developer so inclined could develop a rounded matrix for a system, hence this is not an intrinsic property of the system per se.

Performance

We've shown that the K-O system is easy to apply. But how well does it perform? The comparison tables that follow demonstrate the power of the K-O system.

We note that our rounding of the K-O matrix comes at the expense of expectation. In the "Reduced" comparisons that follow, we will always be adopting the top 16 plays of the K-O Preferred system. Thus, we are comparing the Knock-Out rounded matrices to the unrounded top 16 matrix plays of the other systems, in effect giving the other systems a slight advantage.

Let's restate the benchmarks we will use for the comparisons in this Appendix. Note the slight change in the 6-deck benchmark from that used in the main text of this book (1-8 spread instead of 1-10).

---

[55] The side count, in principle, can be discontinued by a player. Since side counts require so much effort to implement, some may argue that a proper comparison between systems thus should be made without any such extra counts. Qualitatively, the elimination of side counts (for those systems which employ them) comes at considerable expense in expectation. In our comparison, eliminating all side counts would serve to *enhance* the relative performance of K-O and other singular-count systems.

RULE AND BETTING BENCHMARKS

Following are the rules and benchmarks we use to derive the performance results in this chapter.

Single deck: H17, DOA, noDAS, 65% penetration; Spread 1 to 5 with ramp of 3

Double deck: S17, DOA, noDAS, 75% penetration; Spread 1 to 5 with ramp of 3

Six deck: S17, DOA, DAS, 75% penetration; Spread 1 to 8 with ramp of 6

Eight deck: S17, DOA, DAS, 75% penetration; Spread 1 to 10 with ramp of 6

We should mention here that the first edition of *Knock-Out Blackjack* contained a strategy known as the "Core" system. It was similar to this edition's "Rookie" system, only it used a proportional betting scheme and included the proper play of insurance. Because the comparisons that follow are between systems that use proportional wagering, we've resurrected the Core system here.

Let's first consider a 2-deck game with the benchmark rules. We choose the 2-deck game as a compromise between single-deck and multiple-deck games. The penetration is fixed at 75%.[56]

---

[56] See Appendix V for a discussion of the effect on K-O of varying penetration.

SIMULATION RESULTS (EXPECTATION): 2-DECK GAME [57]
(DOA, NODAS, S17, 75% PEN; SPREAD 1 TO 5 W/ RAMP OF 3)

System	Core	Reduced	Full
Knock-Out	**0.86**	**1.14***	**1.23**
Red 7	0.82	1.08	1.12
UZ II	0.85	1.16	N/A
Hi-Opt I	0.80	1.09	1.19
High-Low	0.81	1.08	1.17
Omega II	0.85	1.15	1.28

The Knock-Out value represents the top 16 plays in the Preferred (reduced and rounded) system (Preferred with 18 plays = 1.16; Same 18 plays unrounded = 1.18).

Each entry in this table is based on a simulation of at least several hundred million hands. Perfect play was assumed; no betting or playing errors were introduced. To be fair to each system, we have placed them on the same scale in a modified

---

[57] Following are the sources for all comparisons in this chapter—Red 7: Core adapted from Arnold Snyder's *Blackbelt in Blackjack*; Reduced and Full plays for 1 and 2 decks adapted from Arnold Snyder's "The Big Tilt" article in *Blackjack Forum*, March, 1994; Reduced and Full plays for 6 and 8 decks based on applicable extrapolations from K-O. Unbalanced Zen II: All versions adapted from George C's *The Unbalanced Zen II*. Hi-Opt I: Core and Full adapted from Lance Humble and Carl Cooper's *The World's Greatest Blackjack Book*; Reduced plays are Humble and Cooper's matrix entries for Don Schlesinger's "Illustrious 18" less the two splitting tens plays, hereinafter referred to as the "Sweet 16." High-Low: Core and Full adapted from Stanford Wong's *Professional Blackjack*; Reduced plays are Wong's matrix entries for Schlesinger's "Sweet 16." Omega II: Core and Full adapted from Bryce Carlson's *Blackjack for Blood*; Reduced plays are Carlson's matrix entries for Schlesinger's "Sweet 16."

proportional betting fashion, as described in chapter 7 using full-fractional bet assignments. Note that doing so causes each system to have nearly the same chance of ruin.[58] Also, each system's variation of Core, Reduced, or Full has approximately the same number of strategic plays to memorize that potentially deviate from the basic strategy. The "Core" column, for each system, assumes that the only strategy deviation from basic strategy is the insurance wager.

The "Reduced" column includes only the 16 most significant matrix entries when comparing to the basic strategy. For the unbalanced systems (which behave very similarly strategically), we have adopted the 16 positions that exist in the Preferred form of the Knock-Out system (of course each system has different numerical values as appropriate for the 16 matrix positions). For the Knock-Out 6- and 8-deck simulations, only 14 plays are used. For the balanced systems, we have adopted Don Schlesinger's "Sweet 16" set of the 16 plays which are the most rewarding to memorize.

The "Full" column includes comparisons using 68 plays for all systems. (This is despite the fact that the full-strategy matrix lists only 44 plays.)

As you can see, the systems' expectations are all bunched together fairly tightly. No system's performance stands out as superior over all the rest.

Note in particular that K-O compares admirably with all other systems. Indeed, the two most popular systems in use today, the Hi-Opt I and the High-Low, are both edged slightly by the Knock-Out system. This is despite the fact that the Knock-Out system is vastly simpler to employ.

The Knock-Out system in its most basic forms is such a simple technique that we anticipate many recreational gamblers may want to adopt it. As such, we have included a com-

---

[58] See Appendix VI for confirmation of this statement.

plete comparison table just for the Core incarnations of the various systems below. As always, in each case we have assumed the benchmark rules and betting.

Again, K-O is among the strongest possible systems in performance. This, coupled with its sheer simplicity, makes the K-O Core incarnation very attractive for those wishing to gain an edge over the casino. Today, utilizing the K-O Core system in a single- or double-deck game is probably the easiest method of legitimately beating a casino.

SIMULATION RESULTS:
CORE INCARNATIONS 1, 2, 6 & 8 DECKS

	1 deck		2 deck	
System	Expec. (%)	Ave. wager	Expec. (%)	Ave. wager
Knock-Out	**1.18**	**1.99**	**0.86**	**1.80**
Red 7	1.13	2.01	0.82	1.82
UZ II	1.17	2.05	0.85	1.88
Hi-Opt I	1.12	2.01	0.80	1.80
High-Low	1.14	1.99	0.81	1.81
Omega II	1.16	2.04	0.85	1.86

	6 deck		8 deck	
System	Expec. (%)	Ave. wager	Expec. (%)	Ave. wager
Knock-Out	**0.48**	**1.87**	**0.40**	**1.78**
Red 7	0.47	1.97	0.40	1.87
UZ II	0.48	1.98	0.42	1.87
Hi-Opt I	0.45	1.89	0.39	1.82
High-Low	0.46	1.92	0.38	1.83
Omega II	0.51	1.99	0.43	1.92

As you know, we advocate the Preferred form of the K-O system as the best balance of power and simplicity. Similar arguments have been made for forms of other systems. So for completeness, we present detailed results for a reduced form of each of the popular systems. As before, only 16 ma-

---

SIMULATION RESULTS: 1-DECK GAME
W/ REDUCED STRATEGY
(DOA, NODAS, H17, 65% PEN., 1-5 SPREAD W/ RAMP OF 3)

System	Type	Level	Side count?	Round matrix	Expec. (%)	Ave. wager
K-O	**U**	**1**	**N**	**Y**	**1.53**	**2.09**
Red 7	U	1+	N	N	1.46	2.05
UZ II	U	2	N	N	1.53	2.15
Hi-Opt I	B	1	Y	N	1.47	2.10
High-Low	B	1	N	N	1.47	2.06
Omega II	B	2	Y	N	1.52	2.11

SIMULATION RESULTS: 2-DECK GAME
W/ REDUCED STRATEGY
(DOA, NODAS, S17, 75% PEN., 1-5 SPREAD W/ RAMP OF 3)

System	Type	Level	Side count?	Round matrix?	Expec. (%)	Ave. wager
K-O	**U**	**1**	**N**	**Y**	**1.11**	**1.87**
Red 7	U	1+	N	N	1.08	1.91
UZ II	U	2	N	N	1.16	1.97
Hi-Opt I	B	1	Y	N	1.09	1.87
High-Low	B	1	N	N	1.08	1.87
Omega II	B	2	Y	N	1.15	1.94

trix entries are used for each system.

We note in passing that for multiple-deck shoes, the advantage gained from proper playing strategy is further reduced when compared to single or double decks. A reduced matrix is thus, even more so, the most appropriate vehicle for the

SIMULATION RESULTS: 6-DECK GAME
W/ REDUCED STRATEGY
(DOA, DAS, S17, 75% PEN., 1-8 SPREAD W/ RAMP OF 6)

System	Type	Level	Side count?	Round matrix?	Expec. (%)	Ave. wager
K-O	**U**	**1**	**N**	**Y**	**0.62**	**1.92**
Red 7	U	1+	N	N	0.61	2.04
UZ II	U	2	N	N	0.65	2.07
Hi-Opt I	B	1	Y	N	0.63	1.99
High-Low	B	1	N	N	0.61	1.98
Omega II	B	2	Y	N	0.68	2.10

SIMULATION RESULTS: 8-DECK GAME
W/ REDUCED STRATEGY
(DOA, DAS, S17, 75% PEN., 1-10 SPREAD W/ RAMP OF 6)

System	Type	Level	Side count?	Round matrix?	Expec. (%)	Ave. wager
K-O	**U**	**1**	**N**	**Y**	**0.52**	**1.84**
Red 7	U	1+	N	N	0.50	1.93
UZ II	U	2	N	N	0.55	1.94
Hi-Opt I	B	1	Y	N	0.52	1.90
High-Low	B	1	N	N	0.52	1.91
Omega II	B	2	Y	N	0.57	2.02

best mix of strength and simplicity.

Based on the results from these tables, it's difficult to argue the need for a complicated system. For even in those cases when K-O wins at a slower rate (the product of expectation and average wager is smaller), it isn't appreciably so.

For example, in a 2-deck reduced matrix game, we win at a rate greater than Hi-Opt I or High-Low. And compared to Omega II, we need play only 4% to 5% longer with K-O to achieve the same win. This is roughly the equivalent of playing an extra 10 minutes during a four-hour session. Considering that the incurred stress during a session will be vastly less, you may very well want to stay and play on quite a bit longer than that!

It is true, however, that should you desire to obtain the best possible theoretical expectation, you will need to appeal to the hundreds of matrix entries associated with balanced counts. Unfortunately, in this case, your practical performance may suffer, simply because the extra mental effort required will likely lead to a higher error rate during play.

The effect of errors should not be underestimated. Indeed, it is important enough, and in practice of substantial magnitude, to warrant detailed modeling by some of today's top professional blackjack players.[59]

As we've mentioned before, the K-O system eliminates several potential sources of mental error and mental fatigue. As such, it is quite likely that your win rate with K-O may surpass that of a *theoretically* more powerful, yet also more complicated, system. That is, because of the ease of implementation, your *practical* performance may be superior with K-O.

---

[59] Errors, either by the player or dealer, can result in a significant revenue loss. The MIT team estimates that about 25% of the potential gain from card counting (over basic strategy alone) is typically lost due to errors, even among good card counters.

Appendix IV: The Full Knock-Out System

The "Full Knock-Out" system achieves the system's maximum possible expectation. While we do not recommend this version for most players, we include it here for the record. The only difference between the Full and Preferred systems is that Full has more matrix entries with more numerical values that deviate from the basic strategy. While there's a gain in performance, we don't believe that it warrants the extra effort.

Below is the expectation using the standard benchmarks with the Full system.

K-O FULL

	Expectation (%)
1 deck	1.65
2 decks	1.23
6 decks	0.63
8 decks	0.54

SINGLE DECK
"FULL" MATRIX (STANDARD IRC=0)

Dealer's Upcard

Player's Hand	2	3	4	5	6	7	8	9	10	A
Hard 17 ↑										
Hard 16						8	7	5	1	6
Hard 15						9	9	8	4	7
Hard 14	-1	-1	-2	-3	-3				6	8
Hard 13	1	1	0	-1	-1					
Hard 12	4	3	2	1	2					
11								-2	-1	2
10							-1	1	4	3
9		3	1	0			4	7		
8 ↓			7	6	5	2				

SINGLE DECK
LATE SURRENDER

Dealer's Upcard

Player's Hand	8	9	10	A
Hard 16	5	1	-1	0
Hard 15	6	4	1	3
Hard 14			4	5

Surrender 8,8
vs. a dealer 10 at +2

All soft hands, pairs, and blanks as per basic strategy. Take insurance at running count ≥ 3.

DOUBLE DECK
"FULL" MATRIX (STANDARD IRC=-4)

Dealer's Upcard

Player's Hand	2	3	4	5	6	7	8	9	10	A
Hard 17 †										
Hard 16						10	9	6	-1	8
Hard 15						12	12	10	4	9
Hard 14	-5	-7	-8	-10	-10				7	10
Hard 13	-1	-3	-5	-7	-7					
Hard 12	4	3	1	-2	-1					
11								-8	-7	1
10							-7	-3	3	3
9		2	-1	-5				4	8	
8 ↓			8	6	5	3				

DOUBLE DECK
LATE SURRENDER

Dealer's Upcard

Player's Hand	8	9	10	A	
Hard 16	5	-1	-6	-3	Surrender 8,8
Hard 15	7	3	0	3	vs. a dealer 10 at +1
Hard 14			3	5	

All soft hands, pairs, and blanks as per basic strategy. Take insurance at running count ≥ 3.

SIX DECK
"FULL" MATRIX (STANDARD IRC=-20)

Dealer's Upcard

Player's Hand	2	3	4	5	6	7	8	9	10	A
Hard 17 ✝										
Hard 16							16	10	-8	15
Hard 15										5
Hard 14										13
Hard 13	-13									
Hard 12	2		-2	-7						
11										-2
10									3	4
9			-4					3		
8 ↓					9	5	-1			

SIX DECK
LATE SURRENDER

Dealer's Upcard

Player's Hand	8	9	10	A
Hard 16	6	-13	Su	Su
Hard 15	1	-9	0	
Hard 14	1	7		

Surrender 8,8
vs. a dealer 10 at -2

All soft hands, pairs, and blanks as per basic strategy. Take insurance at running count ≥ 3.

EIGHT DECK
"FULL" MATRIX (STANDARD IRC=-28)

Dealer's Upcard

Player's Hand	2	3	4	5	6	7	8	9	10	A
Hard 17 ↑										
Hard 16									11	-10 . 18
Hard 15										4
Hard 14										16
Hard 13										
Hard 12	1		-5 .	-10						
11										-4
10									3 ...	3
9		-6							4	
8 ↓				10 ...	4 ..	-2				

EIGHT DECK
LATE SURRENDER

Dealer's Upcard

Player's Hand	8	9	10	A
Hard 16	7 ..	Su ..	Su ..	Su
Hard 15		0 ...	Su ..	-2
Hard 14			0 ...	9

Surrender 8,8
vs. a dealer 10 at -5

All soft hands, pairs, and blanks as per basic strategy. Take insurance at running count ≥ 3.

Appendix V: The Effects of Varying Penetration on K-O

Readers familiar with unbalanced counts may be wondering what effect varying penetration has on the performance of the K-O system. Of course, we already know that poor penetration will cost us in terms of performance, simply because favorable opportunities will not arise as often. However, here we are concerned with a subtler effect.

In general for unbalanced counts, if the present running count is between the IRC and the final value, the status of the deck is a function of how many cards have already been played. For example, if we're in a 2-deck game and the count is 0, we *may* have the advantage.

It all depends on how many cards have been played. If we're near the beginning of the pack (where the average running count is near –4), then with our count of 0 we already have the advantage. However, if we're near the end of the pack (where the average running count is near +4), then we are at a disadvantage if the count is only 0.

This may seem a bit confusing because the key count for 2 decks is +1, which implies we're at a slight disadvantage with a count of 0. Remember, though, that the key counts are generated based on a typical penetration of 75% and are derived from the *average* of a large sample of hands. With a count of 0 in a game with 75% penetration, it is *generally* (but not always) true that we are at a disadvantage.

The strategic matrix entry values of *A*, *B*, and *C* were calculated assuming penetrations of 65% for a single deck and 75% for two or more decks. If instead the penetration were different, then the values of the matrix entries may also differ by a small amount.

For example, consider an extreme case where a 2-deck game has only 50% penetration. Then clearly, the running count just before shuffling would typically be near 0 (instead of +2 for the 75% benchmark case). Similarly, the average value for the running count would be –2 instead of –1. As such, the values for *A*, *B*, and *C* might need an adjustment downward as well.

To see the scope of this effect, we have run a test for the robustness of the Preferred matrix. This was accomplished through a simulation of the 2-deck and 6-deck cases where the penetration was fixed at only 65% instead of the usual 75%. As a further test, we have simulated the effects of skewing each of the index entries down by 1 to see what effect this has on the overall expectation. The resulting expectations are presented below:

EFFECTS OF PENETRATION/MATRIX SKEWING ON EXPECTATION

	Penetration	
	65%	75%
2-deck		
Preferred matrix	0.88	1.14
Preferred matrix – 1	0.88	1.13
6-deck		
Preferred matrix	0.43	0.62
Preferred matrix – 1	0.44	0.61

As you can see in the cases with 75% penetration, skewing the Preferred matrix by unity has very little effect on the player's expectation, costing a mere 0.01%. This underscores the fact that the primary gain in the K-O system arises from proper betting rather than playing. It also gives us the "liberty" to further skew the Preferred matrix by a small amount if this makes it somewhat easier to memorize (e.g., see Fab Fives examples in the text).

What is, perhaps, surprising is that even in the case of poor penetration, the additional gain in skewing the matrix numbers is at most a paltry 0.01%. For all practical purposes then, the Preferred system can be played in the form described herein, with almost no strategic penalty in maintaining the standard values of *A*, *B*, and *C* regardless of penetration.

As final evidence that this is true, we have compared the K-O system to the High-Low system in several games with varying penetration. Below is a table in which we show each system's expectation as a function of number of decks and penetration.

COMPARISON OF EFFECTS OF PENETRATION
(75% PENETRATION AND 65% PENETRATION)

System	1 deck	2 decks	6 decks	8 decks
K-O	1.84 1.53	1.14 0.88	0.62 0.43	0.53 0.32
High-Low	1.79 1.47	1.08 0.82	0.61 0.42	0.52 0.32

It is clear that the expectation of the K-O system drops with worse penetration, but the magnitude of the drop is right in line with that from the High-Low system. The High-Low is a balanced system (and "properly" accounts for the number of cards in play) and therefore represents a baseline for measuring the effect of decreased penetration on winnings. That is to say, the drop in expectation for the High-Low system, as a yardstick, reflects the decline in advantage due to betting, as opposed to the strategic play of hands.

Here, however, you can see that each system's expectation declines comparably with decreased penetration. This implies that for the Knock-Out system as well, almost all of the decrease in expectation can be attributed to fewer favorable betting opportunities. This suggests again that the K-O Preferred matrix is appropriate for any reasonable level of penetration, between roughly 60% and 90% of the pack.

Appendix VI: Benchmark Risks of Ruin

One of the reasons that the betting benchmarks for this book were chosen was to place the various systems on the same scale in terms of risk of ruin. Here we use a comparison between the K-O system and High-Low to verify that, indeed, the two systems are equally treated. Below is a table that summarizes the effects of several starting bankrolls, assuming the 2-deck benchmark rules and betting spreads. (We have rounded the results to 1% and 100 or 1,000 hands, as appropriate.)

RISK OF RUIN COMPARISON TABLE
KNOCK-OUT VS. HIGH-LOW

	Risk of Ruin		Average # of Hands to Double	
Bankroll	*K-O*	High-Low	*K-O*	High-Low
500 units	*5%*	6%	*21,000*	22,000
300 units	*15%*	16%	*10,000*	10,000
100 units	*36%*	36%	*1,400*	1,400
25 units	*47%*	47%	*100*	100

As you can see, the two systems' indicators are virtually identical, lending credence to our assumption that the systems have all been placed on the same relative risk-of-ruin scale.

Appendix VII: The K-O for 4 Decks

Following the publication of the first edition of *Knock-Out Blackjack*, we received several inquiries for information about applying K-O in the 4-deck game. It is included here.

The key count for 4 decks is +11 above the IRC. The pivot point is +16 above the IRC. Take insurance, as always, at the count which is one below the pivot point.

Therefore, based on the 4-deck game's standard IRC of -12, the key count is -1, the pivot point is +4, and insurance is taken at +3.

As in 6- and 8-deck shoes, omit Category C plays altogether in the strategy matrix. There are no changes in late surrender.

The expectation for the K-O Preferred for 4 decks (S17, DOA, DAS, 75% pen.) with a 1-6 spread is .75%. The expectation with a 1-8 spread is .95%.

Appendix VIII: Customizing the Knock-Out Count

The standard K-O count can be customized in many different ways. You may want to structure it so that the count points you have to remember for the A, B, and C values in the strategy matrix are always positive numbers, or to eliminate having to deal with negative numbers in the count altogether.

Here's one way that the values can be tailored to suit your preferences. Say you're playing in a 2-deck game and don't want to deal with negative numbers. You can customize to achieve this goal by moving the count reference points around. For example, you can make the pivot point equal to 21 (which is an easy number to remember given the game you're playing).

When you make the pivot point 21 instead of 4, simply modify the other important values—IRC, key count, and insurance—by adding 17 (the difference between the original and the new pivot). So, instead of starting the count at –4 for a 2-deck game, you start at +13 (–4 + 17 = 13). The key count, which was 1, becomes +18. Taking insurance is now correct at +20 (a handy trick to remember is that insurance is always one point below the pivot). We've now set up a system that largely avoids having to use negative numbers. The new values of A, B, and C in the strategy matrix become +21, +18, and +13, respectively.

You can choose any pivot point you desire and modify the references accordingly. Let's say you'd like the pivot to be x instead of the standard 4. Just begin your count with an IRC of $x - (4 \times number\ of\ decks)$; the result will always be $x - 4$ more than the standard IRC. Remember that your new IRC, key count, and insurance count will all be adjusted upward by the same value of $x - 4$. You can also customize with a chosen IRC or key count in mind. Just be sure to adjust the three other reference points by the same number.

Customizing K-O Rookie

A perfect example of customizing the count by a reference other than the pivot point applies to the K-O Rookie system. In K-O Rookie, the key count is the most important reference, so we work from there.

Suppose that your goal is to always have the same key count and also avoid counting in the negatives. Assuming you're using a 1-2 spread, the key count is where you begin to bet two units. So let's fix the key count at "+22." (Easy to remember: Bet 2 at 22.) We know from the table in Chapter 5 what the standard key counts are for 1 through 8 decks, so we subtract the standard values from +22 and adjust the IRC and insurance accordingly (the total number of references drops to three because K-O Rookie does not use a pivot point). Since +22 is 21 points greater, we adjust our two other key references upward by 21.

KEY COUNT FIXED AT +22

	Difference in Key Counts	Standard IRC	New IRC
1 Deck	+20	0	**+20**
2 Decks	+21	-4	**+17**
6 Decks	+26	-20	**+6**
8 Decks	+28	-28	**0**

Insurance changes in the same manner. By adding the key-count differences to the standard insurance number of +3, the resulting insurance points for 1, 2, 6, and 8 decks are +23, +24, +29, and +31, respectively.

Appendix IX: Suggested Reading

We have the pleasure of recommending several fine texts on the subject of blackjack.

Ian Andersen, *Turning the Tables on Las Vegas*, 1976, Vintage Books.

Ian Andersen, *Burning the Tables in Las Vegas*, 1999, Huntington Press.

John Auston, *World's Greatest Blackjack Simulation—K-O Edition*, 1997, RGE Publishing.

George C, *The Unbalanced Zen II*, 1996.

Bryce Carlson, *Blackjack for Blood*, 1994, CompuStar Press.

Michael Dalton, *Blackjack: A Professional Reference*, 1991, Spur of the Moment Publishing.

Peter A. Griffin, *The Theory of Blackjack*, 1996, Huntington Press.

Lance Humble and Carl Cooper, *The World's Greatest Blackjack Book*, 1980, Doubleday.

Don Schlesinger, *Blackjack Attack*, 1997, RGE Publishing.

Arnold Snyder, *Blackbelt in Blackjack*, 1997, RGE Publishing.

Ralph Stricker, *The Silver Fox Blackjack System, You Can Count On It*, 1996.

Edward O. Thorp, *Beat the Dealer*, 1966, Random House.

Edward O. Thorp, *The Mathematics of Gambling*, 1984, Gambling Times.

Ken Uston, *Million Dollar Blackjack*, 1981, Gambling Times.

Olaf Vancura, *Smart Casino Gambling*, 1996, Index Publishing Group.

Stanford Wong, *Blackjack Secrets*, 1994, Pi Yee Press.

Stanford Wong, *Professional Blackjack*, 1994, Pi Yee Press.

Bill Zender, *Card Counting for the Casino Executive*, 1990.

In addition, several excellent blackjack periodicals exist, among them:

Michael Dalton's *Blackjack Review.*
Eddie Olsen's *Blackjack Confidential.*
Arnold Snyder's *Blackjack Forum.*
Stanford Wong's *Current Blackjack News.*

Index

TALE OF THE TAPE

Olaf "Czech's Play" Vancura	VS.	Ken "Unbalanced Kid" Fuchs
33	Age	34
6' 4"	Height	6' 5"
205	Weight	225
45"	Reach	47"
Right	Bats	Right
Sam Adams	Drinks	Miller Lite
Right	Throws	Right
Left	Lacrosse	"Wisconsin town?"
Infinite	Golf Handicap	16
Beantown	Hometown	Windy City
32	Wins	135
5	Losses	12
$1\frac{1}{2}$	Barrings	3
Astrophysicist	Occupation	Electrical Engineer
Numismatist extraordinaire	"Job"	Psychic phone counselor
BSEE, Santa Clara MA, Johns Hopkins PhD, Johns Hopkins	Training	BSEE, Marquette MSEE, Ill. Inst. Tech.
"Another blackjack for you sir! It's a good thing you had that big bet out."	Most Welcome Phrase	"Would you like a rack sir? Your black chips are falling all over the floor!"
"You're welcome to play any OTHER game."	Most Unwelcome Phrase	"Would you like ANOTHER marker sir?"

Ken and Olaf duke it out over royalties.

Great Companions to KNOCK-OUT BLACKJACK:

SOFTWARE SUPPORT FOR THE K-O COUNT BLACKJACK 6•7•8

This awesome blackjack software does everything except pay you when you win. For basic strategy players, it's a tutorial that warns you when you've made a mistake. For card counters, it displays the running count, true count, aces side count, and discards. Allows practice of the Knock-Out count. The program even simulates real-casino conditions with audio and video distractions. This new version is vastly expanded and improved, but it's DROPPED in price. Blackjack 6-7-8 is the best-value software for blackjack players on the market! System Requirements: Windows 95/98/ME/NT/2000/XP; Pentium compatible; 64MB of RAM (128MB, Windows XP); 210MB of free hard-disk space; CD or DVD drive. **$39.95**

• • •

THE THEORY OF BLACKJACK — The Compleat Card Counter's Guide to the Casino Game of 21, 6th Ed. by Peter Griffin   *New Edition! Expanded!*

Griffin's classic work on the mathematics of blackjack provides insight into the methods and numbers behind the development of today's card-counting systems. Now in its sixth edition, THEORY OF BLACKJACK contains the most complete and accurate basic strategy, covering any number of decks, and the most commonly encountered rules. This is the bible for serious blackjack players.

262 pages • soft cover • $11.95 • ISBN 0-929712-13-7

BURNING THE TABLES IN LAS VEGAS, 2nd Edition by Ian Andersen

The long-awaited sequel to Andersen's 1976 best-selling gambling classic, TURNING THE TABLES ON LAS VEGAS. BURNING THE TABLES is the ultimate book on casino comportment and cover play. **340 pages • hard cover • $27.95 • ISBN 0-929712-84-6**

• • •

COMP CITY — A Guide to Free Casino Vacations, 2nd Edition by Max Rubin

Have you ever wondered what it's like to be among the Las Vegas elite who get treated to *free* rooms, gourmet meals, shows, even airfare—all compliments of the casinos? Have you ever dreamed that maybe *you* could get some of the stuff casinos give away to their best customers?

You can! Thanks to COMP CITY by Max Rubin, anyone can take advantage of the secret system the casinos use to determine who gets the freebies, popularly known as "comps."   **382 pages • trade paper• $19.95 • ISBN 0-929712-36-6**

For more information about these and other great gambling products available through Huntington Press, go to :

www.greatstuff4gamblers.com

Huntington Press • 3687 South Procyon Avenue • Las Vegas, Nevada 89103
toll free: 1-800-244-2224 • phone: 702-252-0655 • fax: 702-252-0675

ANTHONY CURTIS' LAS VEGAS ADVISOR Newsletter

The LAS VEGAS ADVISOR is a monthly newsletter devoted to finding the best values Las Vegas has to offer. Each issue covers everything you need to know to get more out of Las Vegas than Las Vegas gets out of you: gambling tips and strategies, casino promotions, tournament and entertainment schedules, restaurant and show reviews, room-rate surveys, advice on finding freebies, and more.

Full Membership ($50US*) includes: 12 monthly issues of the LAS VEGAS ADVISOR newsletter (mailed first-class to your home); 365 days of full access to the lasvegasadvisor.com Web site; the LAS VEGAS ADVISOR POCKETBOOK OF VALUES coupon book (discounts on dining, shows, rooms, car rental, and **gambling**—matchplay, lucky bucks, jackpot bonuses, free aces, and more); FREE LAS VEGAS ADVISOR REFERENCE GUIDE; FREE GREAT STUFF FOR GAMBLERS CATALOG; plus discounts on all new Huntington Press published books.

Online Membership ($37US) includes: 365 days of full access to the lasvegasadvisor.com Web site and the Pocketbook of Values.

Nevada residents add 7.25% sales tax, Canadian residents add $10US, Overseas residents add $20US.

www.lasvegasadvisor.com
or call 1-800-244-2224